*Steve Parish*
PUBLISHING

## A Wild Australia Guide

# LANDSCAPE
## PHOTOGRAPHY

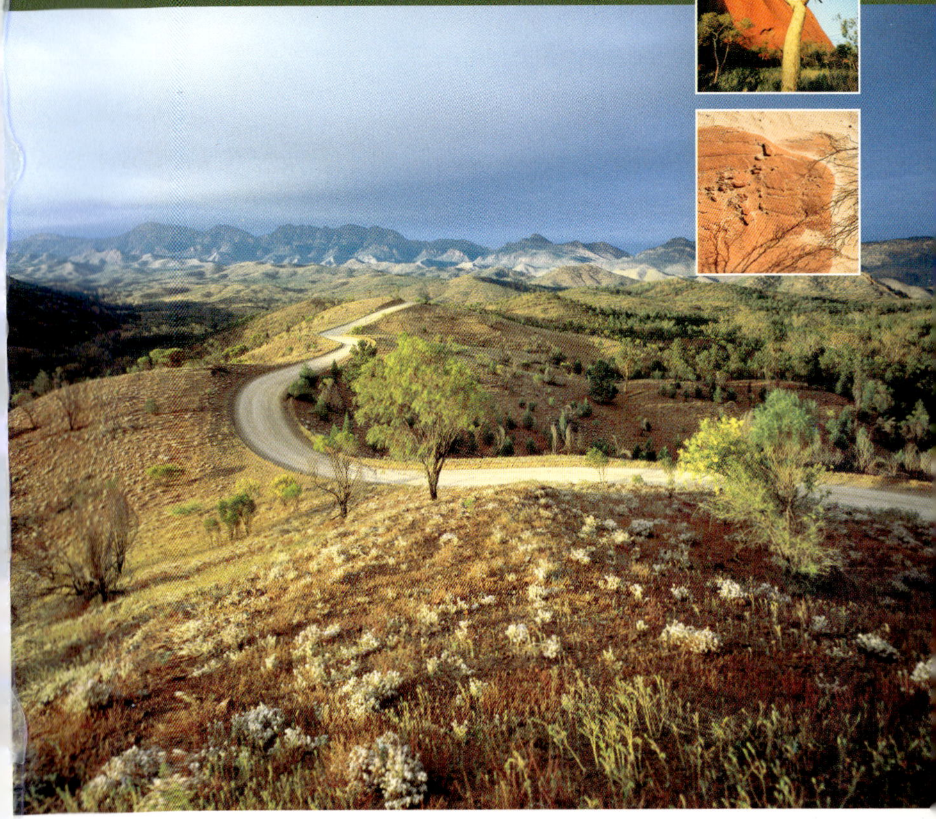

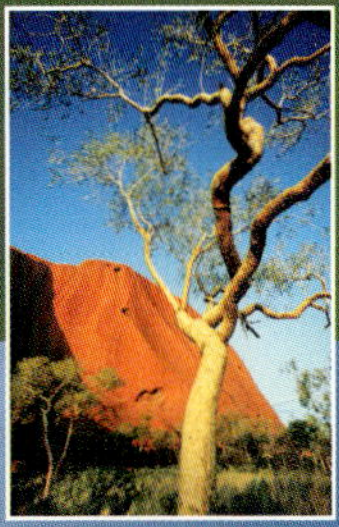

**STEVE PARISH**

# Contents

**Introduction** ... 4
  An SLR or a Compact Camera? ... 6
  Is there a "Right" Lens? ... 8

**The Content of a Photograph** ... 10
  Understanding the Topography ... 12
  Working to a Theme ... 14
  Wildlife & Landscape ... 16
  People in Landscape ... 18
  Plants & Landscape ... 20

**Enhancing the Mood** ... 22
  Australia's Natural Light ... 24
  The Sun ... 26
  Storms ... 28
  Overcast Days ... 30
  Bright Sunny Days ... 32
  Landscape from the Air ... 34
  Sunrise & Sunset ... 36
  Using Light to Convey Feeling ... 38
  Underwater Landscapes ... 40
  Backlighting ... 42
  Twilight Landscapes ... 44

**Designing a Photograph** ... 46
  Horizon & the "Rule" of Thirds ... 48
  Balance ... 50
  The Power of Simple Pictures ... 52
  Lines Lead the Eye ... 54
  Using Shape ... 56
  Framing the Background ... 58
  Managing the Background ... 60
  Creating an Impression
    of Movement ... 62
  Repeating Pattern ... 64
  Varying the Viewpoint ... 66
  High Viewpoint ... 68
  Low Viewpoint ... 70
  Constructing Image Planes ... 72
  Scale & Proportion ... 74
  Cropping ... 76
  Light & Shade ... 78
  Seeking Shadow ... 80
  Silhouettes ... 82
  Angling for Texture ... 84
  Form & Modelling ... 86
  Reflections ... 88
  Does "True" Colour Really Exist? ... 90
  The Feeling of Colour ... 92
  Colour Relationships ... 94
  Dominant Colour ... 96
  Monochromatic Colour ... 98
  The Art of Play ... 100

**After the Field Trip** ... 102
  Digital Manipulation ... 104
  Sharing Your Photos
    on the Internet ... 106
  Audio Visual Presentations ... 107

**Glossary** ... 108

**Index** ... 110

**Online Reading** ... 111

**Opposite:** Rainbow Valley Conservation Reserve *(35 mm DSLR, 14 mm lens, 1/80 f 13, ISO 200 RAW).*
**Above:** Yarra Ranges National Park *(35 mm SLR, 14 mm lens, 1/60 f8, Velvia ISO 100).*

# Introduction

Australia is a wondrous land of ever-changing landscapes. From spacious, open, arid dunes and grasslands with dead-flat horizons to precipitous alpine peaks. These extremes are often only a short drive from urban centres and, with camera in hand, it is easy to get lost in landscape magic. Regardless of the type of camera or lens, the most important factor to keep in mind during landscape photography is content, mood and design. I find the initials "CMD" a useful reminder of these three primary elements.

The content of a landscape scene refers to the land itself and what makes it unique. Are there elements that, if included in a composition, will make my story even more powerful? Mood is a combination of light and other natural environs like mist, rain, clouds, rainbows and so on. Design is multifaceted, involving composition, planes, angles of view and colour. Every time I approach a landscape, I consider all of these elements — as time passes you will find that you will be dealing with these issues subconsciously.

Remembering "CMD" will remind you to capture each place in different styles for different applications. The more you explore landscape with your body, mind and soul — the better you will connect with the subject and, consequently, the more powerful your images will be.

**Top:** There are times when you have to immerse yourself in the landscape.
**Opposite, top to bottom:** Port Campbell's sandstone temperate coast, Vic; Kata Tjuta, Mulga woodland and sandstone massifs, Uluṟu-Kata Tjuṯa National Park, NT; Subtropical woodland bordering perched lake, Fraser Island, South-East Qld; Cool temperate woodlands and forests, south-west Tas *(all photographs 35 mm DSLR, ISO 200 RAW).*

### THE PHOTOGRAPHIC DETAIL CAPTIONS

Where relevant, most captions for pictures provide detail on:
- the format of the camera used (35 mm or medium format, e.g. 6 x 6, 6 x 7 or 6 x 17)
- The viewing system — SLR, DSLR (digital SLR) or rangefinder
- the lens used
- the shutter speed
- the f-stop
- the ISO of the film or equivalent digital setting
- the type of digital file

# An SLR or a Compact Camera?

**Above:** SLR camera

**Above:** Compact camera

It is a natural assumption that the more one pays for a camera the better the pictures will be. This is not the case — people take pictures, not cameras. The higher-priced cameras do have additional features that offer a wide range of alternatives; however, for simple landscape photography these features may not be entirely necessary.

Furthermore, some existing film photographers new to digital photography are tempted to wait until they can afford the "top of the range" digital SLR. This may be a mistake, as many of the lower-priced compact cameras have excellent lenses and a sensor quality to match the higher-priced digital SLRs. For example, one of my associates will only use a compact camera due to its size, weight and ease of operation. He is a naturalist and a nature guide and finds this camera ideal for his pursuits. He uses this type of camera to photograph everything from landscapes to macro close-ups. In fact, his pictures are unique and of such high quality that I publish many in our specialist wildlife books.

Another advantage with many models of compact digital cameras is their live LCD screen. This means you can see your composition, focus and colours as you take the photograph. Some models of compact camera include the rotation of the LCD screen, which enables you to take images in awkward places — close to the ground — without having to lie on it.

Nonetheless, there is no argument that DSLR cameras, offer the greatest range of features. The number and quality of the features on these cameras have expanded extensively in recent times, with new technologies emerging constantly. The quality of the lower-priced models and their lenses has also meant these cameras are now within the reach of most photographers.

### QUICK TIP

**COMPACT OR SLR, WHICH SHOULD I START WITH?** If you are starting out and your objective is to take photographs as a record of your travels and to share online — I would recommend a compact camera. The staff at photographic equipment shops are well versed in regard to the specifications of the equipment they sell and will guide you in deciding on a brand, model and price that best suits your needs. If, however, you are a keen landscape photographer and wish to approach this rewarding pastime seriously, I would definitely recommend a DSLR camera — especially a model that offers at least 8-megapixel resolution.

**Top:** A tripod is a handy tool regardless of the type of camera, although it is especially useful when using longer focal length lenses and slow shutter speeds.  **Above:** During my travels around Australia, I like to take particular note on how people physically use their cameras. I have noticed that for many, couples in particular, the creation of pictures can be a social event. This is particularly the case with a lot of compact cameras because the LCD focus and composition screens allow two people to get involved in the construction of a picture.

# Is there a "Right" Lens?

Following the selection of a format and then brand, choosing a lens, or lenses, can be a big decision — especially for beginners.

The first element to consider is the focal length. Keep in mind lenses are broadly grouped into four categories — wide-angle, standard, telephoto and macro — according to their focal length. It is often assumed that the wide-angle lens is for landscape photography and telephoto lens for objects in the distance. However, this is one of many myths you will discover throughout this book. Any lens can be used for any subject, and your choice of lens' focal length will determine "what it sees". And so, it comes down to what you want your picture to say.

Field (or angle) of view is an important aspect of assessing a lens and is determined by its focal length (for example, 35 mm, 120 mm, 300 mm). Also important is its range of f-stops (apertures, like f 22, f 8, f 5.6) and resolution. This will dictate how much the image can be magnified and the quality when enlarged. Apertures directly affect depth of field. The largest aperture opening (the smallest f number) that the lens will achieve gives a rating for the "speed" of the lens. Lens resolution varies between brands and higher quality lenses are understandably more expensive than lower quality ones. Lens speed (the maximum available aperture) also affects the cost of a lens. Then there are issues of weight. Perhaps auto-focus mode is another choice you would like to have available.

**Below:** A tripod or monopod is essential when using telephoto lenses, especially if you want to be selective with your composition.

**Opposite:** These three photographs illustrate how using wide-angle, standard and telephoto lenses can result in very different shots of the same landscape. While each photograph is of the same range (the Western MacDonnell Ranges in Central Australia), there is considerable difference between each of the photographs in terms of the elements in the landscape that are accentuated. While there are circumstances in which cropping can produce similar results, two primary issues must be considered. Firstly, the size of the enlargement you wish to make. And secondly, the visual effects of foreshortening (the visual compression, or lack of compression) as seen when using wide-angle as opposed to telephoto lenses. While prime, fixed focal length lenses may produce a better result in terms of clarity, there are fine quality zoom lenses that can provide you with many opportunities for variable effects. In short, I would recommend a zoom lens that can range from a wide-angle to a moderate telephoto effect. This means from around 35 mm to 200 mm. The photographs opposite were taken with 20 mm, 50 mm and 750 mm lenses.

### 📷 QUICK TIP

- I would recommend starting with a zoom lens that can range from a wide-angle to a moderate telephoto effect. This means from around 35 mm to 200 mm.

- Remember the higher priced lenses are likely to be of a higher quality. If I am photographing an exceptional landscape scene I prefer to use a prime (non-zoom) lens as the results are always sharper.

# The Content of a Photograph

Content is what you see through the viewfinder — the landform, the vegetation, and the sky. Ask some questions. What is this landscape about? How did it form in the first instance? Is it the geology that has attracted me, or the vegetation, or both? What elements are intrinsically part of this landscape and must be included in my photograph's design? How will mood affect the content? In summary, content lends credibility to an image. It identifies the landscape's position in its total environment. For me, this is the most important consideration — regardless of the mood and the design of the image itself.

**Above and opposite:** These two vastly different perspectives present a lot of information about a unique landscape. The Daintree rainforest is part of the World Heritage Wet Tropics area of North Queensland. To capture the area, many hundreds of images were produced. I have chosen these to illustrate how two images, the landscape and the detail of its vegetation, are often needed to communicate the essence of a landscape *(6 x 7 rangefinder, 43 mm lens, 1/500 f 5.6, Velvia ISO 100; DSLR, 14 mm lens, 1/125 f 16, ISO 320 RAW).*

## 📷 QUICK TIP

- The more you understand the geology and botany of a landscape, the better equipped you will be to interpret it photographically.
- If you can safely wander off alone, solitude can be instrumental in initiating a connection to the landscape you are working in.

# Understanding the Topography

One thing that helps make travel particularly exciting is understanding the topography of an area. For that reason, I have long believed that the more I study topographic maps, the more adventuresome my image-making and travel become. These days of course we have Google Earth, where we can drop in and see the landscape in breathtaking detail — an advantage yes, but I sometimes feel this aid to travel does take something of the mystery out of people's adventures.

Topographical research, regardless of the method, is important for all physical landscapes because it is the topography that determines the climate, vegetation, wildlife and human associations. This is particularly so in Australia, which is a country of startling contrasts. It is these contrasts that often make the scenery even more dramatic.

Overseas visitors, especially those from densely populated urban and industrialised landscapes and even urbanised Australian first-time travellers, are usually quite alarmed, if not overwhelmed, by the sheer size of Australia. The vast open spaces, enormous distances and time it takes to travel from one place to another can even deter them from making a trip. Ensuring that you enjoy your experience is merely a matter of attitude and preparation.

Photographers have the advantage over destination-oriented travellers in that they view every kilometre of the space between destinations as a mini goal in its own right. In fact, if I were to look over my favourite images, I would discover that many were taken on the journeys between targeted destinations. For example, the vast distance across the Nullarbor, or from Port Augusta to Alice Springs, or Alice Springs to Darwin, is rich with photographic opportunities. Never should such a stretch be thought of as a tedious, seemingly endless, time-wasting journey. The fact is that roadside discoveries or short detours can present you with unexpected opportunities. The famous Bungle Bungle Range in north-west Western Australia was unknown (except to Indigenous people) until 1983, when a photographer studied a topographic map and took a detour!

### QUICK TIP

- Consider factoring in extra time to your travel plans — especially during wildflower seasons when birds and insects will be prolific.
- Study topographic maps and even Google Earth when visiting a new area.
- Consider the east–west movement of the sun across your topographic map when making plans. This will assist in saving time when you wish to have the sunrise/sunset paint a landscape with colour.
- The more you study landscape topography and geology, the better equipped you will be when you create your picture stories.

**Above:** One of Australia's many habitats, Sturt's Stony Desert in south-west Queensland was named in honour of the explorer Charles Sturt. During his famous 1844–45 expedition, he was the first European to see it *(SLR, 15 mm lens, 1/125 f 22, Kodachrome ISO 64)*.

**Above:** The weathered domes of the now famous Bungle Bungle Ranges at Purnululu National Park in the north-west of WA are a striking contrast to Sturt's Stony Desert (top). Known to the local Indigenous community for thousands of years, then to cattlemen, this dramatic and isolated range was not launched onto the world stage until it was photographed in 1983. It is now easily recognised on modern topographic maps *(6 x 7 rangefinder, 43 mm lens, 1/125 f 8, Velvia ISO 100)*.

# Working to a Theme

There are five major benefits of conceptualising and photographing to a theme.

Photographic montage is one. By shooting a series of images of one place at one time under similar lighting conditions you will be able to montage or collage your images (tight and loose shots) as one stunning mosaic.

Technical skills can be dramatically improved when you rework a subject repeatedly, I have proved this to myself time and time again. The skills developed through one experience can be used in future shoots.

The reality of commercial value when collecting a "story of pictures" should not be overlooked. To research and experience your "story" in-depth may also inspire you to write a book or an article about it.

The pleasure received from engaging in a landscape is where the spiritual reward comes in. I cut my teeth on seasonal change when I did an eight-season series of trips to Kakadu in the early 1970s.

As your collection grows, you will find the photographs have a greater value in terms of choice and what you are able to offer for commercial sale. For example, if you consider the story of a kangaroo joey's development is worthy of commercial consideration, look beyond just making one image of the kangaroo and her joey. Perhaps the theme of your images may lead you to specialise in the behaviour of kangaroos. As this process unfolds you may start to research, which may lead to putting pen to paper and recording your experiences.

**Opposite and above:** 15 mm, 24 mm, 35 mm and 80–200 mm zoom lenses were all used over a twelve month period to photograph the eight seasons that occur in the Top End of the NT. This was a project I did for Kakadu National Park's interpretive centre and the work was used in an audiovisual presentation. The objective was to paint an aural and visual picture of the dramatic changes that occur throughout the sandstone, woodland and wetland habitats within the confines of the park. This experience left a big impression on me, and even today I try to shoot all habitats in their many seasons.

### QUICK TIP

- A wide-angle zoom and a telephoto zoom are perfect when creating picture stories to enable you to place different emphasis on the same subject quickly.
- Spending time exploring a single theme can heighten your skills and your awareness of the world around you. As such, the rewards are many.
- Variable weather and lighting angles can enhance picture themes by helping make similar subjects look quite different.
- Don't stop shooting when the sun goes down — work with the twilight as well.
- Try under and even over-exposing your photographs. This can enhance the mood by creating a more sinister effect.
- When you work to a theme don't just rely on the pictures as a reference — take notes. As time passes you will find the subtle feelings you had will fade and this will be detrimental to any stories you may wish to produce. It is also important to obtain comments from the locals, as quotes can make a big difference to your story.

# Wildlife & Landscape

Landscape photographs can be particularly appealing when the element of an animal is present in the photograph, even when it is only small. These types of images are also valuable when considering the story. Not from the perspective of landscape photography appeal, but from the point of view of featuring a species' habitat. I tend to think of images that are relatively narrow in their perspective — for example, the cave opposite — more as an element of a landscape. An alternate way of making moderately close examinations of a landscape is to view them as components, or details, or parts of a landscape — they are all relevant to the landscape's story.

Flocks of birds and mobs of kangaroos have great appeal in landscape photography. However, a curious, lone Eastern Grey Kangaroo almost lost in the muted colours of late afternoon can be a useful addition to an otherwise simply constructed photograph of open heathland. In contrast, the appeal of the dark cave in the limestone ranges of southern New South Wales clearly lies in the numbers of bats flooding out of the cave entrance in darkness.

**Above:** A moody afternoon landscape photograph can be greatly enhanced with the presence of birds like these Australian Pelicans. The waterways around Tuggerah Lakes on the Central Coast of NSW provide a perfect western-facing perspective for afternoon photographs like this. By using a telephoto lens I have been able to "pull in" the distant ranges, therefore creating an enhanced sense of place *(35 mm DSLR, 80–400 mm zoom lens, 1/125 f 16, ISO 100 RAW).*

**Above:** Without these Emus, this landscape photograph makes for a very ordinary picture *(35 mm DSLR, 80–400 mm zoom lens, 1/125 f 11, ISO 100 RAW).*

### 📷 QUICK TIP

- If you are using a telephoto lens it is usually best to select your focus point on a single animal and/or the centre of a group of animals.
- When animals are small, a wide-angle lens on a high aperture (i.e. f 22) will give you overall focus.
- While watching the animal for the best posture, don't forget to run your eye around the landscape so that it too is composed in a visually pleasing way.

**Top:** This photograph was taken in total darkness, since lights disturbed the bats. Most of the bats were juveniles with very little flight experience. To focus and compose I arrived early in the evening and set up three electronic flashes and a camera with infrared triggering. Using a head-torch I composed and focused the camera using an ISO of 500 and, with a full-frame digital 14 mm lens set on f 22, I was able to guarantee maximum depth of field. Then it was a matter of sitting in the dark and taking multiple photos in the hope I would capture a number of bats flying out to feed, all in a single frame *(DSLR, 14 mm lens, 1/125 f 22, ISO 500 RAW)*. **Above:** While heathlands in twilight backed by a low mountain range makes a pleasing image in itself, the addition of a kangaroo almost blending into the landscape ensures intrigue *(35 mm SLR, 80–400 mm zoom lens, 1/125 f 5.6, Velvia ISO 100)*.

# People in Landscape

The human form in a wild landscape can be challenging, particularly if the positioning is managed. However, during my career I would describe my better images as those that are more fortuitous than planned. Both the human elements opposite were unexpected — however, both landscape photographs were considerably enhanced by their presence.

The human form in the landscape not only gives scale to the surround, but it can also make a picture more enticing. I tend to use the term "escape pictures" — in other words, eliciting a response from the viewer to want to "escape" to the place portrayed.

**Above:** Isolated from a wide, sweeping landscape at Dove Lake, Cradle Mountain–Lake St Clair National Park, Tasmania — the trail and walkers give scale to the outcrops of rock set in a landscape of heath *(35 mm DSLR, 70–180 mm zoom lens, 1/160 f 6.3, ISO 100 RAW)*.

**Opposite, top:** The great benefit of the presence of the two children at Wave Rock (South-West Western Australia), is they give scale to the size of the unusual geological formation of "the wave". The red tracksuit on the child at the bottom of the pic makes for a nice colour contrast, as does the fact that the two children are bare-footed and competing *(35 mm SLR, 15 mm lens, 1/125 f 16, Kodachrome ISO 64)*. **Opposite, bottom:** Silhouettes, especially when ring-lit, generally offer interesting design elements to work with, and this photograph is no exception. Early morning light across the floodplains of Kakadu National Park is usually a stunning picture in itself; however, the presence of these two figures (one absorbed in photographing) helps boost the appeal of this picture *(35 mm SLR, 80–400 mm zoom lens, 1/125 f 5.6, Kodachrome ISO 64)*.

## 📷 QUICK TIP

- Take care when composing the images and don't forget to shoot verticals as well as horizontals.
- If the human figure is close, decide whether you want the person aware of your presence (looking at the camera), or not. Both can work.
- The addition of spot colour (such as the red clothing of the child at Wave Rock) into a landscape, can add drama to your photographs.

# Plants & Landscape

In the majority of landscape photography shoots, a mixture of geological structure and its associated botany will usually draw your attention in the first place. This is particularly so when the drama of the plants and the quality of the light combine. This was the case with the image below. The light in the field was cold (in other words it had a blue cast) so I warmed it up in post-production digitally. The photograph opposite, however, had perfect light — no additional warming was required.

I tend to approach the plants in a landscape from two directions. Firstly, I may approach the landscape from the plants' perspective — i.e. taking images of the species close-up, I would work backwards to take a photograph of the whole shrub or perennial in situ. Then, I would photograph the landscape where the species grew. The second option is that the landscape will claim my attention in the first instance and then I work the other way in — towards a close-up.

**Above:** The choice of lens focal length, (wide, standard or telephoto) is directly connected to the perspective you want in your photograph. Both the photographs on these pages are wide-angle. The image above, however, has a greater emphasis on the plants — so for this reason I shot from a lower vantage point with a wide-angle lens *(DSLR, 14 mm lens, 1/30 f 16, ISO 320 RAW)*.

**Above:** This image was taken early in the morning, as the sun crept over the sand ridges at Uluru-Kata Tjuta National Park, NT. Three elements make it so stunning. One, the stormy sky to the east. Two, the warm light from the west. And three, my lucky timing — discovering a small area of desert bloom after years of drought *(6 x 7 rangefinder, 43 mm lens, 1/125 f 5.6, Velvia ISO 100)*.

### 📷 QUICK TIP

- Photographing from a low viewpoint (above) or a chest-high viewpoint (opposite) are both relevant when the plants in the landscape are instrumental to the photograph.
- If the plants (shrubs or perennials) are relatively small, a wide-angle lens set to maximum depth of field may be helpful, especially if you wish to include a distant hill or mountain range in focus in the background.
- If the light is low, and a very slow shutter speed is required, use a tripod to add stability.
- Try shooting a variety of images at a range of aperture settings. The metadata embedded in the digital photograph will enable you to study the images later.

# Enhancing the Mood

Mood is a state of mind, the way you think and feel at a particular moment. The most powerful pictures are those conveying a mood to the viewer. Quality of light contributes most to the mood of a picture. It is affected by time of day and time of year, and by particles in the air through which the light passes. These particles are created by rain, snow, wind, haze, mist, fog, dust, pollution and smoke.

In my opinion, mood is the second consideration (after content) in the process of producing a photograph. For example, the mist in the upper left photograph (below) is a primary content of the picture, and it is only when you read the caption that you connect with the location of the picture. Nonetheless, mist is transient, and within an hour it could be gone. Time of day, weather, and season are all-important when you are considering mood. This is why photographers leap out of bed before sunrise and never return to it until the last rays of light fade from the sky.

**Above, clockwise from top left:** A misty, rainy afternoon shrouding the Three Sisters in the Blue Mountains, NSW; Late afternoon under high contrast light; Dawn with morning valley mist; High, midday sun. Each photograph tells its own story regardless of the fact that it has the same subject *(all taken with 6 x 7 rangefinder, 80 mm lens, 1/125 f8, Velvia ISO 100).*

**Opposite:** Sunset paints the Three Sisters in the Blue Mountains with golden light *(6 x 7 rangefinder, 500 mm lens, 1/125 f 5.6, Velvia ISO 100).*

## 📷 QUICK TIP

- Making repeated visits throughout the year is the best way to capture the essence of a landscape in its many moods.
- There is no "right time" of the year or day for landscape photography — any time can be the right time.
- The heads and tails of storms can produce the most dramatic light.

# Australia's Natural Light

Working with Australia's many types of natural light is always a challenge. It can cause aggravation, particularly when all the elements of a stunning picture are in front of you … all, that is, except the "right" light.

Serious photographers spend a lot of time sky-watching, because the sky conditions play an important role in all natural light photography — especially if the sky itself is to be included in the photograph. If the sky is featureless, then you may need to crop a lot of it out by composing the image to include more foreground. Alternatively, empty space can create a great photograph. (You will find that there are few immutables in photography — there are exceptions to most rules.)

In Australia, from the extreme tropical north to the cool temperate south, there is a vast array of weather conditions. Light is directly affected by the weather, which is influenced by topography, latitude, longitude and season.

> ### 📷 QUICK TIP
>
> - Don't fall into the "been there, done that" state of mind. Consider you have never been there before when you revisit a locality. The weather is bound to be different or perhaps you have a new lens to try — you will most certainly be seeing the landscape in a different way.
> - It is only through repetition that we can improve the way we interpret the landscapes we experience.

**Opposite and above:** These photographs were all taken in the same locality, Cape Leeuwin, at the south-western extremity of Australia. Facing west, and with the sun rising from the east, I simply made a series of images with the best of the changing light. The series perfectly illustrates how important it is to revisit the same locality time and time again. It gives the photographer a chance to see a landscape in a different light and to examine the way your skills are developing in the way you see and feel the locality. This can be very encouraging. **Opposite, top to bottom:** Dull and hazy; Impending major storm.
**Above, top to bottom:** Early morning sunny; Cloudy, late afternoon *(all photographs 6 x 7 rangefinder, 60 mm lens, Velvia ISO 100).*

Over the many years during which I have worked with natural light, I have learned to defuse my aggravation and broaden my preparedness to work with varying light conditions. I have discovered that different subjects are best shot in different lights, and that angle of view, choice of ISO (or film speed) setting, lens selection, perspective, and so on, all play a role in shifting emphasis away from "bad" light.

Different kinds of weather suit different kinds of photographic subjects. Overcast weather that doesn't throw dense shadows is ideal for photography inside the rainforest. On a bright sunny day, you might change your plans and head for the coast. If, having arrived at the coast — and before you can unpack your camera, you find that clouds have sprung up and the sky is overcast, go wandering the streets of the coastal town instead.

# The Sun

The sun, source of all natural light — and indeed, of life itself — can make a stunning subject in its own right and can enhance an image through its inclusion within the frame. Composing your photograph to include the sun can create a dramatic effect, especially at sunrise or sunset.

To make an exposure reading when the sun is included in the picture, you have two options. Take a spot meter reading of the sky away from the sun's intense bright centre, or set your camera on multi-pattern metering and the meter will take an average from across the frame. Either way you should be able to make the correct exposure. If you meter directly into the sun with the camera set on centre weighted average, your camera will compensate by dramatically under-exposing — the iris will close to compensate for the bright light. (Do not look directly into the sun, you may damage your eyes.) I tend to take my reading some distance from the sun where the picture may be a little darker. This gives me a more even illumination over the entire image. If I need to make an exposure quickly I will use the multi-pattern meter setting on my camera, which reads and evaluates all areas of the frame.

**Above, clockwise from top left:** Two young children playing at the edge of the sea could not resist pausing to look at the flaming red sunset, Darwin, NT *(35 mm SLR, 600 mm lens, 1/125 f4, Velvia ISO 100)*; A solitary Boab Tree shot against the setting sun in the Kimberley, WA *(6 x 7 rangefinder, 500 mm lens, 1/125 f5.6, Velvia ISO 100)*; When a landscape is as well known as the Twelve Apostles at Port Campbell National Park, Vic, silhouettes can be particularly commanding *(6 x 7 rangefinder, 43 mm lens, 1/125 f8, Velvia ISO 100)*. **Opposite:** Midday is a great time for "into the sun" underwater shots and this image of a Porites coral outcrop was taken at Heron Island, Great Barrier Reef, Qld *(35 mm rangefinder, 15 mm lens, 1/160 f5.6, Kodachrome ISO 64)*.

## 📷 QUICK TIP

- The best way to educate yourself about the emotional interpretation of landscape is to study the works of renowned landscape artists — particularly abstract painters.
- Keep the initials CMD (content, mood and design) in mind. They are the three primary elements that must be considered in the construction of every image you make. Don't let the mood of the setting deter you from checking all the other elements that construct a good image.

# Storms

After a storm — when the sky is spectacular and light gleams through breaks in the clouds — can be a wonderful time to photograph landscapes. Australia has some marvellous storms, especially in the tropics at the end of the dry season. In southern Australia, spectacular cloud formations during inclement weather can appear at any time of the year.

Clouds can often help make a picture, that is otherwise, not much of a picture at all. Some of my favourite images are interesting only because of the sky colours and cloud formations. Rainbows, lightning and the pelting rain are further dramatic elements that can contribute to making a picture stand out from others. When the storm passes there are wet leaves, rushing creeks, dripping ferns and drenched palm fronds. Ah, sweet bliss! These are the elements that make for great landscape images.

**Above:** Wet sand beneath bare feet, the gulls are quiet, and there is only the sound of distant thunder out to sea. These sorts of images cry out for enlargement — they need to be seen in a large format to be appreciated *(6 x 7 rangefinder, 90 mm lens, tripod, 1/30 f8, Velvia ISO 100)*.

**Opposite, top to bottom:** The stunning wet forest of the Tarkine in western Tasmania. This is one of many images I made on a boat trip down the Pieman River. The three-hour boat journey slid past some of the most diverse and spectacular forest I have ever seen. And then it poured with rain, creating a softening filter across the images. I have enlarged this picture as a feature in my bedroom *(DSLR, 80–400 mm zoom lens, 1/125 f5.6, ISO 320 RAW)*; The first storms after a long dry season in Victoria River region, north-west WA *(35 mm SLR, 24 mm lens, tripod, 1/30 f8, Kodachrome ISO 64)*.

## 📷 QUICK TIP

- Carry a very large umbrella so that you can photograph from beneath it.
- Stormy grey clouds, with gaps that let sunlight through, can also be effective. In these situations the sun's rays can also add to a picture's appeal.
- If you are taking a walk in wet weather it is always wise to carry camera protection, even if its only a humble plastic bag.

# Overcast Days

When light cloud cover is diffusing the light, don't despair. This can be exactly what is needed for many landscape situations. Fine particles in the air soften the harsh rays of sunlight and, in certain circumstances, this can enhance the mood in an image. I find misty and hazy days particularly beneficial for close-up or telephoto work with wildflowers and wildlife, or when shooting inside a forest or around waterfalls. In these instances, dark shadows that can ruin a photograph can be gently filled in. The waterfall opposite is an excellent example of filtered sunlight filling in shadows. An added benefit of cloudy weather is to provide more visible detail in vegetation and on rocks.

Another effect of diffused light is to intensify colour. This effect can be sometimes improved when bright areas of sky are excluded from the frame, although sometimes, as seen on the opposite page (top), cloud cover can form part of the picture. The form of a subject is also more likely to be enhanced in diffused light, especially if the photographic angle is right. To select the best angle, simply try moving around your subject.

**Above:** An overcast day is perfect for photography inside a rainforest — note the shadow detail *(6 x 7 rangefinder, 43 mm lens, 1/60 f 16, Velvia ISO 100)*.

**Opposite, top to bottom:** This was not the weather I wanted. However, the repeating pattern of the cloud, plus water reflections and intensified colours combined to make this picture both a great illustration of a floodplain, and a very appealing photograph *(6 x 7 rangefinder, 43 mm lens, 1/60 f 16, Velvia ISO 100)*; A hazy day was the right time for an aerial photograph of Jim Jim Falls, which lies on the western edge of the Arnhem Escarpment in Kakadu National Park, NT. On a sunny afternoon the shadows would have been dark *(35 mm SLR, 80–400 mm zoom lens, 1/15 f 5.6, Kodachrome ISO 64, from the air)*.

### 📷 QUICK TIP

- If a hazy sky is bright and white you could consider either lowering the horizon in your composition or cropping the sky out altogether.
- The best way to take light meter readings on hazy days is to point the camera down towards the ground, eliminating the bright sky.
- I usually employ multi-pattern automatic light meter readings and lighten dark areas in the picture during post-production.

# Bright Sunny Days

The main problem associated with photographing towards the middle of a bright sunny day can be high contrast between light and shade. This may produce deep, dark, unattractive shadows with little or no visible detail, and colours with little tonal variation — though this is not always the case, as varying quality of light can produce such different effects.

Earlier in my career I avoided photographing under these conditions, preferring to photograph only in the softer warmer light of early morning and late afternoon. However, I have found that if I work throughout the day, carefully choosing my subject, lens and angle of view, I can extend my working time.

**Above:** A bright sunny day adds to the "beach flavour" of this image from North Stradbroke Island, Qld *(6 x 17 rangefinder, 43 mm lens, 1/125 f 16, Velvia ISO 100)*.

**Opposite, top to bottom:** High sun can be effective around beaches and coral islands. It is usually when the sea is at its bluest, and the sun's vertical rays penetrate clear water to create a "can't wait to dive in" impulse *(6 x 7 rangefinder, 43 mm lens, 1/125 f 16, Velvia ISO 100)*; There are occasions when you have no choice but to photograph when the sun is high. For example, you may not have the opportunity to tour Katherine Gorge at the best time to take advantage of the early or later afternoon light. In this case, you will not want to miss opportunities just because the light is not at its best *(6 x 7 rangefinder, 43 mm lens, 1/125 f 16, Velvia ISO 100)*.

### 📷 QUICK TIP

- A small aperture results in increased depth of field, which means a handheld camera doesn't need a tripod and foreground objects, like rocks on a beach, will be crisp in focus.
- Bright sunny weather allows higher shutter speed, which are great for freezing action within the landscape.
- Light penetrates the surfaces of water best when the sun is high in the sky so this can make natural light for underwater landscapes more colourful.
- Photographing in gorges with parallel high walls is another circumstance when high sun can create better photographic results.

# Landscape from the Air

The primary advantage of photographing from the air is that you are able to get perspectives that are not possible on the ground. To a great extent, the effect of light on landscape from overhead, whether from an oblique or vertical perspective, is much the same as on the ground. The main difference is that distant haze can be more accentuated. However, it does depend on the distance from the subject and the density of particles in the air.

Apart from UV filters, and the odd occasion when I use a Polaroid filter to remove water reflections, I do not use any filters. Digital cameras make it possible to increase the ISO rating and therefore the shutter speed. With my D3 camera I can comfortably shoot at 1000th of a second on an ISO of 400 on a bright sunny day. Even with smaller compact cameras you will find adjustments to ISO and therefore increased shutter speeds are easily managed.

**Above:** Overcast weather can be excellent for landscapes that, on a sunny day, may have harsh, dark, shadowed areas *(35 mm DSLR, 14 mm lens, 1/500 f8, ISO 320 RAW)*.

### 📷 QUICK TIP

- Plan your trip to make the best use of lighting, making sure that you have the best seat down-sun from your flight path. Remember, if you are chartering the plane or helicopter, you are the boss. Unless your requests are unsafe, you will find that the charter pilot will cooperate.
- Where there is shadow, try and shoot obliquely so as to give depth and dimension to your shot — an example is shown opposite, bottom.
- Study the light for a few days before you charter a flight, this will assist in choosing the best time of day. Unless the pilot is a photographer, don't assume he or she will know best.
- It is important to request either an open window or a door taken off. Shooting through Perspex does not produce clear results.

**Above, top to bottom:** There are thousands of people who climb the Hazards at Wineglass Bay, Tasmania, in an attempt to photograph this famous beach. Most are disappointed to discover that while the view is stunning, it does not let you to take a photograph of the whole beach. A few kilometres to the north however, one can charter a plane and create an image just like this *(6 x 7 rangefinder, 43 mm lens, 1/500 f8, Velvia ISO 400)*; The famous Bungle Bungle landscape of sandstone domes is a favourite with landscape photographers. From a ground perspective the extensive coverage of massed domes is hard to capture *(6 x 7 rangefinder, 43 mm lens, 1/500 f8, Velvia ISO 400)*.

# Sunrise & Sunset

In the glow of many sunrises and sunsets, colours are usually warmer than during the day. However, the air temperature is cooler, making it more likely that wildlife will be out and about.

Haze is welcome at these times of day for the additional drama it can add (opposite, above and below). The angle of the rising or setting sun can also produce some spectacular sky colours that are often reflected tonally through the picture. Your photographs may be of any kind of landscape, from deserts to coasts. At dawn, the sun's rays may have to penetrate fog, which produces wonderfully soft images. At sunset, the day's dust reflects the fading light and softens the world's hard edges.

Water, wet sand or wet mud reflections can also add to the drama of the scene and, depending on your angle of view to the sun, there may be some fine silhouettes that can be included in your compositions.

**Above:** This image was taken early in the afternoon as the sun — sinking to the west — began to render the landscape in a golden-yellow hue. Geiki Gorge National Park, the Kimberley, north-west WA *(6 x 7 rangefinder, 43 mm lens, 1/125 f 5.6, Velvia ISO 100)*.

### 📷 QUICK TIP

- Don't forget to examine the landscape away from the sunset as grasses, shrubs, trees, rocks and distant ranges will be reflecting the sky colours (see above).
- If there are large dark areas in the photograph you may choose to bracket your photographs, although these manipulations can also be done on your computer.
- If there has been wind during the day, it may suddenly drop off as the sun begins to set. This is the best time for water reflections.

**Above, top to bottom:** A view from the Twelve Apostles lookout, on Victoria's south-west coast. During the last three hours of daylight, blankets of sea mist wrapped the sandstone coast *(6 x 7 rangefinder, 43 mm lens, 1/125 f 5.6, Velvia ISO 100)*; The wetlands of the Townsville Town Common — facing west with distant mountain ranges — make an ideal setting for wetland landscape photography at sunset *(6 x 7 rangefinder, 500 mm lens, 1/125 f 5.6, Velvia ISO 100)*.

# Using Light to Convey Feeling

There are occasions when the light contributes substantially to the overall message that you want to convey when you are making pictures. For example, blue natural light in the background of underwater pictures immediately takes the viewer to that world. A bright blue sky and red sand will transport an audience directly to the desert, even though there may be little visual information in the picture to communicate locality.

The photo-essay on these two pages was recorded in Kakadu National Park in the Northern Territory. Even though there is nothing to suggest Kakadu specifically, there is plenty of information to say "tropical", and when grouped together they take the viewer to this "other" tropical world. What I want to convey by grouping them together might be little more than "this is a special place". The colour tones are evocative and act as a balm to the spirit. In my experience as a photographer, I have found that these sorts of soft muted tones do evoke people's emotions.

**Above:** Pandanus by the sea *(6 x 17 rangefinder, 90 mm lens, 1/125 f 5.6, Velvia ISO 100).*

**Opposite, top to bottom:** Floodplain at sunset, Kakadu National Park, NT *(35 mm SLR, 15 mm lens, 1/125 f 5.6, Kodachrome ISO 64)*; Floodplain and sandstone at dawn, Ubirr, Kakadu National Park, NT *(35 mm SLR, 135 mm lens, 1/125 f 5.6, Kodachrome ISO 64)*; Originating in the sandstone country of the Arnhem Escarpment in Kakadu National Park, NT, the South Alligator River snakes its way across vast floodplains to the sea *(35 mm SLR, 35 mm lens, 1/125 f 5.6, Velvia ISO 100, reflecting twilight)*.

## 📷 QUICK TIP

- Although page 92 deals with the effect that various colours can have on our mood, I have another tip for you. One way to heighten the mood of your image is to collage your pictures. This can be done on a page, or in a picture frame or in a series of frames decorating a room.

- Conveying a feeling through your image will be intensified during periods of mist, light rain, dawn and dusk light. Twilight and even bushfire smoke can add drama to a picture.

# Underwater Landscapes

When I photograph underwater I like to carry two cameras — one for close-up work, and another with a wide-angle lens for reef scapes. The reason for always toting a camera specifically for natural light is that naturally lit underwater photography is a most challenging, yet highly effective form of photography. Underwater colours range through all shades of blue and green. Working in naturally lit conditions, I look for dramatic reef shapes, preferably where I can include the lighter surface of the ocean. This means looking up for shots rather than down. It also helps to work in shallower water.

Visibility is best on a day of clear blue skies and calm water, at midday when the sun is high overhead. Dive at either the bottom or top of the tide to get the best clarity, especially near the coast in shallow waters. If the water is murky when you dive, reduce the camera-to-subject distance by working as close as you can to the subject.

Photographs begin to take on a blue cast at depths of just a few metres. This is because the water selectively absorbs the light wavelengths. Shorter red wavelengths from sunlight are the first to go, causing reds to appear either very dark brown or black at around 10–15 m. Orange disappears at around 20 m, yellow at around 30 m, green at around 40 m and blue turns black at around 50 m.

**Above:** At around 10 m, the corals take on a distinct blue cast. Remember, you do not need to invest in expensive underwater photographic equipment to try your hand at this exciting form of landscape photography. There are many inexpensive packages now available for cameras, flash units and underwater housings that will see you in action for a moderate investment *(all photographs 35 mm rangefinder, 15 mm lens, Kodachrome ISO 64)*.

## 📷 QUICK TIP

There are four primary causes for light loss underwater:

- Weather conditions above the surface — overcast skies will reduce underwater visibility.
- The position of the sun — if the sky is clear and the sun is directly overhead, then the light path is more direct and light, and thus visibility, is at its clearest.
- Reflection off the water's surface — if the surface of the water is rough, then light will break up and will not afford the same visibility as when the surface is calm.
- Suspended particles causing light to scatter — the water can become cloudy with little more than a shift in tide when sand or other matter is stirred up.

**Above:** The main picture illustrates how having the sun directly overhead is best for clarity. However, even at this shallow depth the colour of the corals are muted due to the influence of the sunlight.
**Left:** This image illustrates how bringing artificial light (an underwater flash) below the surface can counteract the light absorption effects of the water — to highlight the beautiful colours of the corals.

# Backlighting

Positioning yourself so that your subject is between you and the sun will present what is known as backlighting. Depending on the angle of light, the focal length of your lens and your viewpoint in relation to the subject, some very stunning images can be achieved. Backlighting gives not only depth and dimension to a picture, but seems to confer a three-dimensional look on vegetation due to its translucence (below).

Constantly studying the sky is an absolute must, especially if unique and unusual lighting is something you want in your photographs. Backlighting may be achieved when the sun is hidden, even on bright overcast days. All that is required to capture the effect is a bright source of light behind your subject. If you find the sun flaring, position your angle of view so that the sun is just "tucked" behind foliage, a tree branch or a rocky outcrop (opposite).

While these sorts of images can be very appealing, it is important to be careful with exposure reading. My rule of thumb for determining the exposure is to ask myself what it is in the picture that is of primary interest. I then usually take a centre-weighted or spot meter reading on that selected point of interest. In the case of the photograph opposite, I would meter the shaded areas of the tree trunk.

**Above:** Late afternoon backlighting in the Warrumbungle National Park, NSW has far more appeal than front lighting *(6 x 7 rangefinder, 43 mm lens, 1/125 f 16, Velvia ISO 100).*

### 📷 QUICK TIP

- If you make an error with your metering and underexpose, you can always lighten the dark areas in your photograph using software on your computer.
- I like to use the centre-weighted metering adjustment on my SLRs, being sure to meter in the main areas of shadow. This will give detail, for example, to the trunk of a tree or the shrubs in your picture.
- Backlit images, particularly medium close-ups like the one opposite, do have far more depth and dimension when backlit. Direct front lighting can easily flatten a landscape picture.

**Above:** There will be many times when you will have little or no choice but to use backlighting — wanted or not. I was collecting a series of the gorges along the MacDonnell Ranges for a project and found that to achieve the "right light" for all would have taken ten days. Here, in Ormiston Gorge I "tucked" the hot sun behind foliage to reduce lens flare, and exposed the shadow side of the tree trunk *(35 mm DSLR, 150 mm lens, 1/125 f16, ISO 100 RAW)*.

# Twilight Landscapes

Twilight — when the sun is below the horizon but its light can be seen — occurs in the morning just before sunrise and in the evening after sunset. The word is most commonly used during evening. The available light is from light rays that illuminate "sky particles" (matter such as dust, ash, or water in the form of mist or cloud). At dawn, the light first filters across the sky before the sun rises over the horizon.
At sunset, after the sun has sunk below the horizon, the sky colours remain until overcome by the ink-blackness of night. Because the sun's rays are oblique and the "sky particles" act as minute reflectors, the colours looking towards the sun are more intense. And how intense depends on the amount and density of clouds and other reflective particles. Colours may appear so surreal that viewers assume coloured filters have been used. Heavy, dark clouds on the horizon at dawn may completely ruin twilight effects and, at sunrise, I have waited with great anticipation only to have dark clouds scud across the sky at exactly the wrong time.

Camera shake can be a problem during the long exposures required in low light situations. To overcome it, use a tripod with a cable release or set the self-timer for a 2–5 second delay. Then, as long as the subject is not moving, you will be able to reduce shutter speed quite considerably. If the subject is moving, use a faster lens (a fast lens is one designed for such circumstances and it has a small f-stop number such as f 2.8 or f 1.2) or an even faster film. Increasing the ISO setting on your camera is another solution. You can do this on individual frames with a digital camera.

**Above:** Mudflats in north-west WA reflecting a twilight sky *(35 mm SLR, 105 mm lens, 1/500 f8, Ektachrome ISO 400).*

## 📷 QUICK TIP

- Landscape photographers are often accused of "pumping" their colours when twilight photographs are in public view. This is because non-photographers do not usually register these often-surreal colours.
- Most subjects, including birds, flowers and people, can be photographed under twilight conditions.
- The modern digital camera with low noise levels at a high ISO rating has, under many conditions in the field, illuminated the need for long exposures and, therefore, tripods.

**Above:** Both snow and rocks on this alpine peak in Kosciuszko National Park, NSW, reflect the western colours of evening twilight *(35 mm SLR, 50 mm lens, 1/60 f4, Kodachrome ISO 400)*.

# Designing a Photograph

While in the field, photographic design falls into four primary areas — picture composition, planes and views, light, and colour. Understanding how to manage and arrange these areas will assist with the design skills that can be developed simultaneously with your own personal technique. The reward is the sheer joy of finding your very own style as a photographer of landscape.

Photography is a journey and every picture is a product of the moment — whether arranged or spontaneous. What you see and feel, and how you interpret a scene or subject today will almost certainly change tomorrow. I am always looking to improve composition, and hence the power of a picture, to effectively communicate with the viewer. I am always wanting to feel that I am progressing in both my skills and perceptions.

**Above:** Simplicity juxtaposed against complexity is what makes this picture interesting and a favourite landscape photograph of mine. My challenge was to capture the naked dunes, those with vegetation and the vastness of the surrounding landscape in the Simpson Desert, Qld *(35 mm SLR, 80–400 mm zoom lens, 1/125 f16, Kodachrome ISO 64).*

**Opposite:** Don't forget to give yourself permission to play with your camera. The Finke River, Central Australia, NT *(35 mm SLR, 35 mm lens, 1/500 f8, Kodachrome ISO 64).*

### 📷 QUICK TIP

- As you let your imagination run free, your creativity will begin to fire. Then, who knows what can happen!
- Film types and formats, camera brands, accessories and so on, are the means of taking images, not the ends in themselves.
- There are many books on design in art that are directly applicable to photography.

# Horizon & the "Rule" of Thirds

Many people don't need rules. Their results have a natural balance and order. I endorse the philosophy of Peter Emerson, the 19th century photographer who was the first to promote photography as an art in its own right. He advocated that each photograph requires its own composition free from the restrictions of formulas.

Nonetheless for the beginners, I have indicated some approaches that may be helpful in your early exploration of design. These are guidelines only, to be broken, modified, played with and adapted. Some of the common pitfalls in composition are centering the main subject where it is most visually boring, leading the eye out of the photograph, and failing to adequately isolate the main subject. However, these "faults" can be used to telling effect. Remember that strict adherence to the compositional rules may ultimately stifle creativity. The aim is to take photos that are pleasing to the eye and evoke emotion.

## HORIZON

Horizon in a picture is connected to aesthetic appeal. However, there is a mathematical relationship to design that works around the Greek Golden Mean (the desirable middle between two extremes) in western culture. Most people can intuitively see the appeal of a well-balanced picture without going into the detail. It is useful to understand this relationship and then push yourself to photograph in a different way. The picture at top is composed with a high horizon giving emphasis to the foreground. The centre image gives equal emphasis to sky and foreground and the lower image highlights the sky. There is no right or wrong, it is all about personal appeal. Of course if you shoot your pictures a little "loose" you can play with your cropping when you are back home on your computer *(6 x 7 rangefinder, 43 mm lens, 1/30 f 16, Velvia ISO 100, tripod)*.

## RULE OF THIRDS

A rectangle is divided into thirds horizontally and vertically, and the elements of the picture — focus points, horizons, subjects — are arranged along the lines and intersections of the grid (below). The central picture shows the grid. The picture at bottom shows a different composition. Is one composition better than the other?
*(DSLR, 14 mm lens, 1/10 f 16, ISO 320 RAW, tripod).*

# Balance

Balance is the art of placing the elements of the composition into an arrangement, either harmoniously, in conflict or with a detached eye for the best result. Each element has its own weighting compared to other elements in the frame. By altering viewpoint, lighting and focal length, it is possible to create many arrangements of elements and, thus, different compositions.

There is formal and informal balance. I usually avoid the formal, which is symmetrical, preferring the more interesting informal, or asymmetrical balance. Informal balance may involve elements of similar shape and size or different shape and size. It is with these variations in mind that we compose our photographic images.

To achieve balance in a photograph, imagine the subjects sitting on a seesaw, placed either equidistantly (formal balance) or at unequal distances (informal balance) from the fulcrum, the point at which the seesaw pivots and to which the eye is drawn. A good composition achieves balance around a focal point in the photograph. Just as on a seesaw, the "weightier" subject needs to be closer to the fulcrum to balance a "lighter" subject further away.

Having learned about all these guides, use them as just that — guides. They are not carved in stone, and in some cases may be better ignored.

### CREATING BALANCE

In a picture with many elements and detail, it is still possible to create a balance. The bush in the foreground near the large tree trunks acts as the pivot between the large trees and the smaller bushes combined with the mass of the hills in the background.

## SYMMETRY OR FORMAL BALANCE

The image is almost formally balanced, almost symmetrical, befitting the subject.

## INFORMAL BALANCE

Balance is created between asymmetrical but similar subjects by ensuring that the pivot point, the eye focus point, is close to the larger subject in order to maintain the balance of the two elements. The overall composition of the picture is then aesthetically pleasing.

# The Power of Simple Pictures

Regardless of whether a landscape is complex or simple in its structure, the ultimate challenge is to compose it so that it communicates effectively. A simple picture may combine two or three elements, yet have striking shape, line or colour. In contrast, complex images, full of distractions, may be harder to decode visually purely because of their large amounts of visual information. Sometimes, enlargement can help in these circumstances.

To better understand the power that simplicity has, flick through the pages in this book and see which shots are memorable, or run your eye across book jackets in a bookstore and see which ones draw your attention. You will be quite amazed by the way simple design can stop you in your tracks. Browse your image collection and you might find that your favourite is the uncluttered, clear composition that emphases only a few of the elements of colour, form, texture, or shape.

So how do you simplify a complex scene? Vary the lighting, selectively compose by changing lenses or, more importantly, vary your viewpoint. In some circumstances, it is possible to simplify a picture after cropping it, by focusing on a particular element that has created it.

**Above:** Snow-covered peaks, rocky ridges, cloud shadows and a storm laden sky — why include anything else *(6 x 7 rangefinder, 43 mm lens, 1/400 f 8, Velvia ISO 100, airborne)*.

### 📷 QUICK TIP

- Time, a relaxed state of mind, and solitude (collectively) are three basic ingredients that will help you move away from making ordinary pictures to creating images that simply demand attention.

**Above:** High-impact elements — line, texture, pattern and the complementary opposites of red, white and blue — are what makes this image visually demanding *(35 mm SLR, 15 mm lens, 1/125 f22, Kodachrome ISO 64)*. **Left:** First light over Stirling Ranges National Park, South-West WA *(35 mm SLR, 600 mm lens, 1/125 f5.6, Kodachrome ISO 64)*.

# Lines Lead the Eye

Lines in image construction — perhaps more than any other element — can be used to steer the viewer's eye towards, into, out of, or even away from the main centre of interest. Diagonal lines in particular have dynamism. In some cases, repeating lines merge into the world of pattern, but they can continue to steer the eye. Care is needed to present the lines without too much other distracting detail in the same picture. Line and perspective are linked — strong lines in a picture may lead the viewer to make assumptions about depth and distance, and may guide the eye to the focal point of a picture.

To arouse people's interest in sharing your journey, the lines should convey a sense of motion. An S-curve through a scene will evoke the experience of wandering through a restful country area. A river meandering into the distance has a similar effect on the viewer.

The best time to plan to use lines in composition is when you're in the field looking through the camera's viewfinder, although adjustments may also be made when you are cropping a developed image. Line, like texture, colour, shape, and so on, is an exciting design element available to the imaginative photographer.

**Above:** The tapering lines in this photograph of the sandy cliffs of Peron Peninsula, WA, take your eye past the beach walker, down, and out of the picture *(6 x 7 rangefinder, 43 mm lens, 1/125 f8, Velvia ISO 100)*.

**Opposite, top to bottom:** Once a living coral reef, this dramatic limestone range snakes its way across the flat lands of the southern Kimberley. The curving line of the range and the billabong take the eye on a journey *(6 x 7 rangefinder, 43 mm lens, 1/500 f8, Velvia ISO 200, airborne)*; Accentuated by shadow, sand lines move the eye to the end of the beach on Green Island, North Queensland *(6 x 7 rangefinder, 43 mm lens, 1/125 f16, Velvia ISO 100)*.

### 📷 QUICK TIP

- Lines will lead the eye just as train tracks vanish into the distance. Ask yourself when you are composing your picture where you wish to lead the viewer — away into the distance, left or right, or up into the sky.

# Using Shape

Identifiable shapes — domes, cones, pinnacles, spheres and so on — make powerful and often alluring photographic subjects, either independently, or as elements within a landscape composition. To accentuate shape, and support its strength in communicating directly with the viewer, it is important to see it in relation to its immediate surrounds. This is especially true when there are other elements present such as background, lighting, or even other surrounding shapes that might dilute the impact.

In order to achieve a clear result, carefully choose the viewpoint. As you move around, ponder on the various angles because shape distortion can add or detract from the effect you are wishing to convey. It is also important to consider the angle and quality of the light.

**Left:** Stones, a strip of Mulga woodland and the distant domes of Kata Tjuṯa, Uluru–Kata Tjuṯa National Park, collectively make this image a powerful story told through shape *(6 x 17 rangefinder, 90 mm lens, 1/60 f 22, Velvia ISO 100)*.

## 📷 QUICK TIP

- Your choice of lens, from ultra-wide-angle to very long in focal length, can also radically alter perception of the shape.
- Shapes need not be isolated to make an arresting photograph. Keep your eye out for shapes forming distinctive repeating patterns.

**Above, clockwise from top left:** One cone of the Three Sisters, Blue Mountains, NSW *(6 x 7 rangefinder, 500 mm lens, 1/125 f 5.6, Velvia ISO 100)*; Sandstone pinnacles, the Lost City, NT *(6 x 7 rangefinder, 43 mm lens, 1/500 f 8, Velvia ISO 100, airborne)*; Magnetic ant mounds, Litchfield National Park, NT *(6 x 7 rangefinder, 43 mm lens, 1/125 f 16, Velvia ISO 100)*; Nambung National Park, WA *(6 x 7 rangefinder, 43 mm lens, 1/125 f 16, Velvia ISO 100)*.

# Framing the Background

A powerful and extremely effective way to compose a picture is to frame the primary point of interest with other surrounding elements. Framing is another way to present the arrangement of the various elements in front of you. To achieve the best result, you might have to change your lens or change your position, as you would to find the best viewpoint.

In the natural environment, vegetation and rocks provide perfect frames. The concept of framing the background for effect should not be restricted to the traditional approach. The edge of the picture itself is a frame and the choice of where to crop the scene or subject is influenced by the message you wish to communicate. The other distinct advantage of this approach to constructing your images is that it helps tell a story with great effect — as is obvious in the surrounding photographs.

**Above:** Native Pandanus trees are common along the coast of Qld. Here, on North Stradbroke Island, I have used a dip in the vegetation to frame Main Beach *(6 x 17 rangefinder, 90 mm lens, 1/125 f 16, Velvia ISO 100)*.

**Opposite, top to bottom:** The Natural Arch at Springbrook National Park, Qld, is framed from inside the cave, adding drama and depth *(6 x 7 rangefinder, 43 mm lens, 1/125 f8, Velvia ISO 100)*; Uluru, Uluru–Kata Tjuta National Park, NT, is at the top of the list for travelling landscape photographers. Here, from the walking track, I have framed a section of the monolith with a tree. The oblique, golden light of late afternoon adds warmth and has created shadows that give form and depth to this stunning scene *(35 mm SLR, 15 mm lens, 1/125 f8, Velvia ISO 100)*.

## 📷 QUICK TIP

- A wide-angle lens is not essential when framing; you can use any lens, even a very long telephoto lens. In the latter case, the foreground elements would need to be distant, rather than close.
- Depth of field (the areas in focus from the distant point of interest to those used to frame the background) is a primary issue with framing.

# Managing the Background

I have always taken the approach that the background of a picture is as important as the subject's main centre of interest. I apply this to all subjects, from close-ups to landscapes. The background of a picture may be either the place where the eye finishes its journey, or alternatively the agent that draws your eye back to the centre of interest. In some cases, the centre of interest and the background work as one (the grass-tree opposite is an example).

There are many techniques for managing the background. You can change camera perspective (lower or higher), wait for weather to change, adjust orientation (horizontal to vertical), adjust horizon position, employ depth of field (blur background), take a higher or lower perspective, or physically move your shooting position so as to rearrange the elements in your picture.

**Above:** Mist can be a very effective way of enhancing the background of a landscape picture, especially a forest *(6 x 17 rangefinder, 90 mm lens, 1/15 f22, Velvia ISO 100, tripod).* **Left:** The drama of twilight added to this shot of Hamersley Range, WA *(6 x 7 rangefinder, 43 mm lens, 1/15 f16, Velvia ISO 100, tripod).*

**Above, top to bottom:** This solitary grass-tree was studied in full sun and then photographed the following morning *(35 mm SLR, 15 mm lens, 1/15 f 22, Velvia ISO 100, tripod)*; By composing to give emphasis to the foreground of this Phillip Island seascape, I have effectively managed the background *(6 x 7 rangefinder, 43 mm lens, 1/15 f 16, Velvia ISO 100, tripod)*.

### 📷 QUICK TIP

- If you can camp on your landscape you will be able to better take advantage of the passing weather and lighting conditions.
- Remember you can make many changes to your backgrounds (you can even change them altogether!) during post-production using your computer.

# Creating an Impression of Movement

Depicting motion is a very exciting challenge in photography, and there are times when this simple addition is all that is needed to make an otherwise ordinary picture simply stunning.

If you select a high shutter speed, say, 1/1000th of a second, then the subject will be pin-sharp and appear as though frozen in time. If, however, a slow shutter speed is used, say 1/5th to around 1/30th of a second, then any movement within the frame will appear blurred. The level of blurriness corresponds with the slowness of the shutter speed.

When the camera is panned during slow exposure, this will create an effective depiction of motion. If you are panning to follow something, like a running kangaroo, then the subject will be sharp and the background will be blurred.

The pictures opposite were both shot the same way. I simply put the camera on a tripod and selected a slow shutter speed. This gave me sharp surrounds and blurred action within the frame.

**Top and opposite, top:** To create a sense that water is flowing, I usually select a shutter speed between 1/5th and 1/15th of a second. If the light is too bright to achieve a slow speed, a neutral density filter may provide a solution *(6 x 6 rangefinder, 60 mm lens, 1/15 f 16, Velvia ISO 100).*

**Opposite, bottom:** The seeming movement of the waves enhances this simple, yet dramatic picture *(35 mm SLR, 15 mm lens, 1/15 f 22, Kodachrome ISO 64).*

## 📷 QUICK TIP

- Try selecting a slow shutter speed and moving your camera in a variety of ways during exposure. Apart from the possibility of creating some stunning abstracts, this will help you to learn the kinds of effects that are possible.

- Don't forget that impressions of movement can also be created during post-production in Photoshop. You will find blur tools under "view" in Photoshop.

- Shoot in the early morning and late afternoon when light is low. This will assist you by allowing the selection of slower shutter speeds.

- Remember to make lots of variable images by adjusting your shutter speeds.

- Waterfalls, swaying tree branches and so on are best made with the camera on a tripod. This ensures that the primary areas of the landscape are nice and sharp.

# Repeating Pattern

A harmonious pattern, composed of similar elements, may represent order and concord — making a picture pleasing to the eye and to our innate sense of organisation. A discordant pattern, composed of dissimilar elements, may make our senses reel. Pattern is composed of line, shape, colour and repetition and these elements may exist in a composition in conflict or in harmony. You will find that patterns abound and although pattern may be just one element of the overall picture, it can be at its most effective when isolated.

**Above:** Wetlands, Mary River Park, NT *(6 x 7 rangefinder, 43 mm lens, 1/60 f 16, Velvia ISO 100)*.
**Left:** Spinifex-covered dunes at Uluru–Kata Tjuta National Park, NT *(SLR, 80–200 mm zoom lens, 1/126 f 5.6, Kodachrome ISO 64)*.

### 📷 QUICK TIP

- If you look, you will find pattern, simple and intricate, everywhere — in fallen leaves, fields of flowers and ripples in sand.
- While filling a composition with identical objects that form a pattern, it is also possible to include additional elements and retain the success of the images. The images above, and opposite top and bottom are examples where the patterns are enhanced by additional elements.

**Top:** Fitzgerald River National Park on the central south coast of WA is without doubt one of the most inspiring wild landscapes in Australia. Here, after an extended period of strong winds, I accentuated a vast area of continuous pattern through the use of a wide-angle lens and a high horizon *(6 x 7 rangefinder, 43 mm lens, 1/60 f 16, Velvia ISO 100)*. **Above:** Karri forest at Walpole–Nornalup National Park, WA *(6 x 7 rangefinder, 500 mm lens, 1/60 f 16, Velvia ISO 100)*.

# Varying the Viewpoint

When looking at a scene with the naked eye, you soon become aware of the amount of peripheral information that surrounds the area of primary interest. To overcome this, look through the camera's viewfinder that isolates the area of interest with the peripheral information cropped out. Next, start considering which of the relationships between the elements now visible in your viewfinder you want to feature in your picture.

Often, you might not have a specific idea in mind — much like an artist developing sketches before making a final painting. You look at a series of images, varying your viewpoint as you go. As you move through and around a scene you will be amazed at how each composition, when analysed, has a different story to tell. You could choose a high viewpoint by standing or climbing something, or a low viewpoint by squatting or lying on the ground. You may even choose to move in close or attach a telephoto lens. The variables are only as limited as your imagination. The photographs opposite were all taken in one locality and while they are only four of the several dozen I made, they do represent the primary options that were available.

Colour can be affected by the angle of view and hence colour tone is particularly apparent when you are shooting towards the sun. The decreased exposure may plunge elements of an image into either total black silhouette or much darker tones than those recorded by the human eye.

**Opposite and above:** All images are of Arthur Range in Southwest National Park, World Heritage Area, Tasmania. They were taken in exactly the same locality and by simply changing lenses I could — with little physical movement — isolate elements in the broader scene and record images that present totally different sets of information *(lenses are clockwise from top left 200 mm, 14 mm, 750 mm and 600 mm, all images DSLR, ISO 320 RAW)*.

### QUICK TIP

- Even if you don't have a series of lenses, (let's say you have one 50 mm fixed lens on a compact camera), it is still possible to produce a number of different photographs of a particular scene. It is simply a matter of changing your viewpoint. Up, down, with foreground, without foreground and so on.

- Varying viewpoint is akin to play. A child with a crayon sets out to draw an imaginary scene by making numerous marks on a piece of paper. Their hand and their imagination are working in coordination. The child wants what they see in the mind's eye to appear on the paper. The marks on the paper continue and in time the child stops and holds up the paper to show the teacher while expressing a sense of satisfaction. What are they satisfied with exactly? With having successfully drawn what was imagined. That's exactly what I am talking about. Picture what you want and play with your camera until you get it!

# High Viewpoint

In certain circumstances, a landscape is best photographed from a high viewpoint, in other circumstances it is merely an option. For example, while both the landscapes opposite are dramatic from a low viewpoint, they are both considerably more dramatic from a higher vantage point.

Even by the roadside I often use my roof rack to give me a more elevated perspective. There are times when roadside vegetation is too high and this slight elevation assists with the composition. Of course there may be a pile of rocks or even a mountain to climb that gives you a series of differing viewpoints.

**Above and right:** Port Campbell National Park, Vic — under the right weather conditions the numerous viewpoints from the boardwalk do provide exciting views; However, if you climb down Gibson's Stairs to the beach below, the viewpoint takes on a whole new challenge *(6 x 17 viewfinder, 90 mm lens, 1/125 f 8, Velvia ISO 100).*

**Opposite, clockwise from top:** Tasman Island Lighthouse from a helicopter with the Tasman Peninsula in the background; Tasman Island Lighthouse from water level *(both images DSLR, 14 mm lens, 1/500 f 8, ISO 320 RAW)*; Viewed from a cliff-top walk, a tour boat heads out for a day of adventure on the Katherine River at Nitmiluk National Park, NT; A less interesting viewpoint of the Katherine River from water level *(both images 6 x 7 rangefinder, 43 mm lens, 1/125 f 16, Velvia ISO 100).*

### 📷 QUICK TIP

- Learn to think outside the square, to take photographic risks.
- Images that don't work for you today may tomorrow. Nonetheless you can always delete images.
- If you are commercial, do the work and then play. I find that nowadays I use more of my "play pictures" than the commercially driven pictures I used to worry about.

# Low Viewpoint

Before realising there are alternatives, photographers may confine themselves to photographing from a standard front-on point of view, usually in a standing position. It can make a collection of photographs appear dull and boring. One way to dramatically change your approach is to take photographs from a low viewpoint. Depending on the subject, this departure from the normal perspective can result in strong visual impact because the view has moved from being ordinary to out-of-the-ordinary.

**Left:** A big challenge! How do you photograph an entire tree in the middle of a forest landscape? In this case I had no option but to get down among the litter and mosses and take a low viewpoint *(35 mm DSLR, 10 mm lens, 1/30 f 22, ISO 320 RAW)*. **Opposite:** If the subject is large, like the sandstone domes opposite, photographing up from a low viewpoint creates a looming effect. The lower picture, highlighting the river pebbles, tells a slightly different story *(both 6 x 7 rangefinder, 43 mm lens, 1/60 f 22, Velvia ISO 100)*.

### 📷 QUICK TIP

- Getting down on the ground is a wonderful way to connect with a landscape.
- When you shoot low be sure to examine both the vertical and horizontal perspectives. Even if you prefer one or the other you may change your mind when in front of the computer.
- Wide-angle lenses, having a greater depth of field, are best used for low-angle photography.

# Constructing Image Planes

An important area of photographic design is the effective creative management of the foreground, middle ground and background information within a picture. Collectively these are known as the image planes. Not all pictures will have them, nor do they necessarily need them to work. Nonetheless, photographs that do express image planes are more likely to hold your interest.

The image can lead the viewer's eye through these three image planes in a variety of ways, depending on how you construct the image. What is important is to select a lens and viewpoint that ensures each plane is clearly visible, while making sure one is not obstructing or conflicting with another. It may require a slight adjustment of your viewing position, perhaps as little as a few centimetres.

You will find that the majority of images contain foreground, middle ground and background image planes and it is the combination of these elements that give an image dimension.

**Top:** Even in a panoramic photograph, image planes are relevant. Nambung National Park, WA *(6 x 17 rangefinder, 90 mm lens, 1/125 f8, Velvia ISO 100)*.

**Opposite:** Three photographs taken on the same morning stroll on Lord Howe Island all employ the same compositional foreground, middle ground and background image plane principals. One talks about the volcanic geological construction of the island, another about the desire to escape, and the other suggests escape of a different kind *(all images opposite taken with 6 x 7 rangefinder, 43 mm lens, 1/60 f 16, Velvia ISO 100)*.

## 📷 QUICK TIP

- There are no rules — each image varies with the elements it contains.
- Using a tripod helps you to carefully construct images, giving you time to reflect on what you are doing. Try a lightweight fibreglass tripod.
- Image planes should be considered regardless of cropping and orientation.
- The foreground in particular can assist you in telling a story with your image.

# Scale & Proportion

The scale of a subject refers to its size, and its proportion as seen in comparison with another subject. With this in mind, the scale of a subject can be managed — in fact it may be crucial for the viewer to be able to understand the comparative sizes of the subjects. This of course has its variables and is directly connected to your own needs to communicate. In my own work I find I need images with and without references to scale and proportion.

**Above:** A viewer would have no reference as to the sheer size of this dune on Fraser Island, Qld, without the car *(35 mm SLR, 80–400 mm zoom lens, 1/125 f 16, Velvia ISO 100)*. **Right:** The enormity of these Karri Trees in Shannon National Park, South-West WA, is quickly made evident by the road and car *(35 mm SLR, 80–400 mm zoom lens, 1/125 f 5.6, Kodachrome ISO 64)*.

### 📷 QUICK TIP

- By using a tripod and a self-timer shutter release you can always add yourself as "the scale reference".
- My rule is always to add "known" objects if they are available. For my publishing work these sorts of images have entirely different applications.

**Top:** A hazy day at William Bay National Park, South-West WA, has greater appeal due to the addition of a solitary figure *(35 mm SLR, 80–400 mm zoom lens, 1/125 f16, Kodachrome ISO 64)*. **Above:** The sheer scale of Kings Canyon Gorge at Watarrka National Park, NT, is highlighted by using a human silhouette *(6 x 7 rangefinder, 43 mm lens, 1/125 f16, Velvia ISO 100)*.

# Cropping

While lenses and angle of view can be changed to adjust composition (crop pictures) in the field, remember that when you do create optical changes and angle variables you may also be dramatically changing the perspective of your images.

Cropping is a function performed either in the field with the camera or at home on your computer (or in the laboratory if the image is to be developed as a print). You may have achieved what you wanted in the field when you took the photograph, but cropping an image at a later date may convey a different concept altogether. If you are selling the images to a library, or you have performed the photographic task for a client, then cropping may be done by a designer who uses the image on the required product. Give them options and they will remember your work with favour.

**Above:** There are some landscapes that provide several cropping opportunities. There are others that are perfect the way they are. Remember that you can crop your pictures simply by changing lenses, however you may not think of that at the time or it may be inconvenient *(6 x 7 rangefinder, 60 mm lens, 1/125 f8, Velvia ISO 100)*.

### 📷 QUICK TIP

- While you may be the art director when you take your pictures, try to remember that you won't enjoy that control in a commercial sense. So always keep the alternatives in mind.
- A vertical or panoramic picture may be cropped from a traditional horizontal, as shown opposite.
- When I make a series of images on a subject, I usually ensure that at least a few frames are loosely composed to give me more leeway for cropping to utilise for my publishing business.

Before I "went digital", I preferred to make my landscape images with a 6 x 7 medium format camera. This not only gave me the enlargement detail I needed, but also enabled me to crop my images — often quite radically. Now that I shoot digitally I am able, with careful management, to obtain very similar results.

**Above and left:** Although shot under lightly overcast conditions the saturation and detail in this image of Kata Tjuṯa, at Uluṟu-Kata Tjuṯa National Park, NT, has been used many times as both a full-frame and also with several different crops *(6 x 7 rangefinder, 60 mm lens, 1/125 f 5.6, Velvia ISO 100)*.

# Light & Shade

Making use of light and shade can give the two-dimensional photograph the illusion of being three-dimensional, contributing depth to an image. Light and shade may also accentuate colour and contrast and, when managed during composition, direct the viewer's eye. The more effectively this is controlled, the more dramatic an image can be. Light and shade exist in most photographs and their subtle variations can communicate a considerable amount of information as subtext in a photograph. I think of light and shade as tools in the photographer's bag of tricks that can be used in the "management" of the viewer's response to our images.

**Above:** The light and shade on this massive Boab in the Kimberley District, WA, is responsible for the impact of this picture *(6 x 7 rangefinder, 43 mm lens, 1/125 f 16, Velvia ISO 100)*.

### 📷 QUICK TIP

- To manage and manipulate light and shade, a photographer must consider time of day (and therefore the angle of the light from the sun), and the angle of view.
- The effect of light and shade can be enhanced simply by changing the direction (angle of view) from which you approach the subject.

**Top:** This image of a dry river bed in western NSW was taken in the late afternoon light. Without the light, shade and the golden glow of the afternoon it would not have been a picture worth taking *(6 x 17 rangefinder 90 mm lens, 1/125 f 5.6, Velvia ISO 100)*. **Above:** Without some light and shade areas, snow-covered mountains appear flat and without form *(6 x 7 rangefinder, 43 mm lens, 1/125 f 5.6, Velvia ISO 100)*.

# Seeking Shadow

Shadows, either as a minor part of the picture or as the main feature, are often essential in creating a sense of depth. There is no "best" time of day, however early and late in the day shadows are usually accentuated.

A pale and preferably flat background gives contrast to a shadow and adds drama. You may choose to accentuate the shadow by under-exposing your photograph by a half to one full f-stop. If your camera is manual, this task will be comparatively straightforward. If your camera is automatic, you might try adjusting the ISO setting one or two stops higher.

You will often find that the shadows in your images play a less-dominant role than the main subject, but they should not be ignored — the effect they represent may be very important in bringing the whole picture together.

**Left:** Wave Rock, a unique sandstone geological feature in South-West WA, is given a heightened form by shadow *(35 mm SLR, 15 mm lens, 1/125 f 5.6, Kodachrome ISO 64)*.

### 📷 QUICK TIP

- Varying your angle of view will either accentuate or diminish areas of shadow.
- Shadow can be used to frame a landscape, giving a heightened sense of depth. The shadowed areas of the landscape opposite almost act as a door inviting the viewer to enter.
- A less recognised role for shadow is that it can accentuate the lighter areas — as seen in the image above.

**Above:** Every time I see this photograph I am reminded that I should always take more advantage when the light is perfect. In this situation, I am presented with what I would describe as idyllic light. The shaded foreground, the light spilling down through the forest, and onto the creek creates an overall desire to escape down this apparently calming corridor found on Fraser Island. In all, this is a delightful construct of the elements. I have since revisited this locality a dozen times and have never seen lighting circumstances that even vaguely compared to this time *(6 x 7 rangefinder, 60 mm lens, 1/125 f 5.6, Velvia ISO 100)*.

# Silhouettes

When a subject is backlit, the usual rule in photography is to expose for the point of primary interest, ignoring the overall background. In some situations it may be more pleasing to reverse the situation and expose for the background, as is the case with the pictures on this page. The most dramatic results are achieved when the subject is simple and has a distinctive shape, effectively drawing the eye to it as the primary centre of interest. These sorts of images make excellent enlargements and look quite dramatic framed and hung on your wall, particularly when the background colours are appealing — such as soft pastels or even sunset or twilight colours.

You will find that potential subjects abound. What is important is that the overall shape is compelling in some way. Graceful curves or humorous shapes work well.

**Above:** At Cape Hillsborough National Park, Qld, an Eastern Grey Kangaroo visits the tideline to cool off. The rising sun has created a silhouette *(35 mm SLR, 80–400 mm zoom lens, 1/400 f 5.6, Velvia ISO 100).*

**Opposite, top to bottom:** Depending on your angle of view, mountain ranges or monoliths like Uluru and Kata Tjuta, can present graduating shadows which are very effective in the creation of a sense of depth in a picture *(35 mm SLR, 80–400 mm zoom lens, 1/1000 f 5.6, Kodachrome ISO 64)*; Beside the road at Hotham Heights in the Alpine National Park, Vic, I was taken by the juxtaposition of the pure white snow and the branches of burnt trees which are the result of the January 2003 fires *(6 x 17 rangefinder, 90 mm lens, 1/125 f 5.6, Velvia ISO 100)*; The Gammon Range, SA *(35 mm, 80–20 mm zoom lens, 1/125 f 5.6, Kodachrome ISO 64).*

## 📷 QUICK TIP

- It's the expression of your imagination through the way you put together all the variables that makes a picture powerful.
- As you can see on these pages, the silhouette does not have to be the only area of interest.

# Angling for Texture

The texture in a photograph is influenced primarily by the direction of light and the surface texture of the subject. The quality of the light is also an important factor. Soft, oblique, golden light can enhance an image and this is shown in effect in the image of Nature's Window (below).

The best result is achieved when light creates a three-dimensional effect giving the sense that, if you touched the surface of the photograph, it would feel as it looks.

You will find textured surfaces almost anywhere, particularly in nature where they abound in rock surfaces, tree bark, leaves, and sand. Close-ups can be dramatic, so next time you are on your hands and knees in the bush, take a close look. The position of your camera determines your angle of view and that angle, in relation to the light direction, is what increases or decreases the dimensional effect of texture.

### 📷 QUICK TIP

- Moving your camera shooting position will readily reveal increases and decreases in the textural effect. Simply select the one that suits you best.
- Late and early oblique light works best for texturally enhanced photographs.

**Top:** Late afternoon oblique light has heightened the texture in the sand here at the Flinders Ranges, SA *(6 x 7 rangefinder, 43 mm lens, 1/125 f 5.6, Velvia ISO 100)*. **Above:** The oblique light of early morning has created a three-dimensional effect across the heathlands of the Stirling Range National Park, in WA *(35 mm SLR, 80–400 mm zoom lens, 1/125 f8, Velvia ISO 100)*. **Opposite:** Nature's Window, Kalbarri National Park, WA. Photographing from the right angle, in late afternoon oblique light, gives an added textural "feeling" to this photograph *(6 x 7 rangefinder, 43 mm lens, 1/125 f8, Velvia ISO 100)*.

# Form & Modelling

Silhouettes and shadows are generally perceived as two-dimensional because they focus on the subject's outline. Form and modelling, on the other hand, create a third dimension, giving the subject volume. When you are photographing a still life in controlled lighting, even if you use flash, the variables can be tested and moved individually for effect. If however, your subject is immoveable, your viewpoint must change to vary the effects. Regardless of whether the light is soft or harsh, at early morning or after sunset, it is the angle of the light in relation to your viewpoint that creates the form and modelling within your photograph.

**Above:** Just the right angle to photograph the true form of Uluru. Most photographs that we see of this stunning monolith give the impression the surface is relatively flat *(DSLR, 35 mm lens, 1/125 f 16, ISO 100, RAW)*.

**Opposite:** This grand Ghost Gum, at Trephina Gorge National Park, NT, is said to be the largest in the MacDonnell Ranges. See how movement around the tree towards the shadowed side has given the tree trunk an accentuated form *(DSLR, 14 mm lens, 1/125 f 16, ISO 100, RAW)*.

### 📷 QUICK TIP

- High sun can induce hard, dark shadow, so sometimes slightly overcast or hazy weather is the best to form a graduated shadow which will enhance the form of a subject.

- If I am working through an area, I try to arrive at a particular time of day, such as in the morning. I make those images that are best suited to the available light, taking mental notes about alternative subjects that may be better around noon, or later in the afternoon. I will then return.

# Reflections

Any smooth surface will produce reflections but in the natural world, water is the most obvious source. Wet sand, mud and water surfaces, calm or smooth, all produce varying degrees of reflection. Even a small variation in your angle of view can enhance or reduce the desired effect of a reflection, especially when you are working close to your subject, so it is important to investigate various angles of view before you start shooting.

Exposure will only be an issue if the reflection includes very bright highlights. In these instances it is best to take your meter reading manually, cropping the bright area out of the picture. Then, with exposure set, move back and re-compose the photograph ignoring the meter needle that may be jumping off the scale.

**Left:** Here the early, warm light reflects along the edges of dark volcanic rocks on Ball Bay, Norfolk Island *(6 x 7 rangefinder, 43 mm lens, 1/15 f 16, Velvia ISO 100, tripod)*. **Below:** Late afternoon light paints the normally grey limestone walls of Geikie Gorge National Park, north-west WA, with golden light. The still, slow-flowing water in turn creates a wonderful reflection *(6 x 7 rangefinder, 43 mm lens, 1/15 f 16, Velvia 100 F, tripod)*.

### 📷 QUICK TIP

- One of the fascinating aspects of reflection is that the human eye will accept distorted reflections as long as the source is included in the photograph. Cropping out the source of the reflection can produce an interesting abstract image. You may confuse or even excite the viewer.

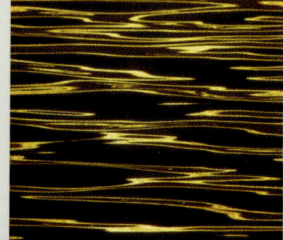

**Top:** A delightfully formed billabong at the Northern Territory Wildlife Park, Top End, NT *(DSLR, 14 mm lens, 1/125 f11, ISO 200, RAW)*. **Above:** Cape Hillsborough National Park, Qld, has a very shallow sloping beach which is perfect for reflections at low tide *(6 x 7 rangefinder, 43 mm lens, 1/60 f11, Velvia ISO 100)*.

# Does "True" Colour Really Exist?

Probably the most important thing to appreciate with colour photography is that colours are dependent on light conditions. Light is affected by particles in the air — water (rain, snow, clouds etc.), or other matter (industrial pollution, smoke, dust etc.) — as well as the time of day, which governs the amount of atmosphere the light has to pass through. When these factors coincide with the physics of light, then light is reflected, scattered, diffused, refracted, polarised and absorbed, thus altering the apparent colour of a scene.

As well, the trueness of the colour will depend on the colour bias of the film and the effect of filter or lens optics. Or, with digital cameras, it could also depend on the white balance and the tint or hue adjustments set on your camera. If an image is lithographically printed, then the variation in colour may be enormous because, as each image is scanned, the person operating the scanner interprets its colour. Then it is passed through a machine that employs chemically based colours and this process makes yet another interpretation of what the true colour should be. Next time you see a caption under a picture that says "natural colour" or "true colour", you can be assured that unless the subject is close-up and artificially lit, then the colour will not necessarily be true — but it can be quite natural. The colours in a photograph should ultimately be what is pleasing to the eye, and what appears to be natural, based on what is known as "retained colour memory."

**Above and opposite:** These photographs taken from Hamilton Island, although varying slightly in composition, were all taken from the same viewpoint towards Goold Island National Park, Nth Qld. There was approximately 30–40 minutes between each shot. The series illustrates how colours can change dramatically, especially during the periods of dawn and dusk *(6 x 7 rangefinder, 43 mm lens, Velvia ISO 100).*

### QUICK TIP

- If you are photographing landscapes, then ultimately the colour of the final print that pleases you is the one to select.
- If you deliberately set out to create colours in scenes that are far from how they appear naturally, you may cause viewers to reject the image. Alternatively, experimenting with colour may result in a creative piece that could have a positive effect on a viewer.
- The essence of colour is to enjoy and experiment with it in your photography.

# The Feeling of Colour

In nature photography there is no such thing as good or bad colour. Chosen colour combinations are a matter of personal perception and subjective appreciation.

Significantly, we often use the same adjectives to describe colours as we do to describe feelings and personality traits — loud, boring, bright, lively, bland, or exciting. One of the most interesting areas of the study of colour as it relates to how we perceive it, is the significance of a colour, and its relationship to other colours in different cultures in our world. For example, in some Western cultures women marry in white, which symbolises purity, while in some Eastern cultures white symbolises death and mourning.

We make colour choices every day. The clothes we wear, the space we live and work in, even the car that we drive. The colours of clothing are largely managed by the fashion industry whose income depends on predicting the trends. A colour that is in fashion this year may be "out" next year. Some people have their colours "done" by a person who advises them on the best colours to wear according to hair, eye and skin tones. People also prefer wearing particular colours. Mine is blue, but I also love white, particularly when I am tanned. The contrast makes me feel attractive.

**Above:** Sometimes nature presents us with an array of complementary yet quite different colours, such as during a seasonal event like flowering *(DSLR, 14 mm lens, 1/125 f6, ISO 100 RAW)*.

### 📷 QUICK TIP

- Experiment with colour in your photography and don't be afraid to work outside the "acceptable" square. And don't forget your post-production where you have the ultimate control over colour.

- Colour in a photograph can be enhanced by the selective choice of mats and frames. You may like to experiment on your computer before you go to the framing gallery.

**RED** is physically stimulating and may be perceived as lively and exciting — or demanding and aggressive.

**BLUE** encourages intellectual activity and will calm the mind or stimulate thought, depending on the intensity of the particular hue. It can also be perceived as cold and unfriendly.

**YELLOW** supports optimism and creativity, encouraging confidence and a sense of wellbeing. Negatively, it can upset those who are emotionally fragile, with low self-esteem.

**GREEN** is at the centre of the spectrum and is therefore considered restful. It is also a very reassuring, balanced colour. It can, however, be perceived as too bland and slightly nauseating.

**VIOLET** takes the mind to a higher level and encourages reflection and meditation. It can create an insular environment or feeling.

**ORANGE** combines physical energy with mental qualities. It can enliven the emotions, and create a sense of wellbeing. It can however, also be associated with tension, tiredness and depression.

# Colour Relationships

Another fascinating aspect to consider when creating colour images is how the various colours relate to each other. If composed carefully, images with intense colour, even those having little variation in light and shade, can have lots of impact. As in all forms of successful communication, less is more, so the power of an image might decrease as more colours are introduced. You may notice when you flick through these pages that the images which have the most effect on you, are those with two main contrasting colours.

The colours of strongest contrast are those that lie opposite each other on the colour wheel (opposite). They are termed complementary colours. Blue (primary colour) is opposite and complementary to orange (red + yellow, secondary colour), red (primary colour) to green (blue + yellow, secondary colour), and yellow (primary colour) to violet (blue + red, secondary colour). An image becomes particularly powerful when colour relationships are working and, depending on the content, its message will be conveyed most effectively.

**Above:** Here at Shark Bay, Peron National Park, WA, the contrasting colours of the desert dunes against a vivid blue sky provide opportunity for startlingly coloured landscape photographs, especially in the late afternoon when the colours are warm *(6 x 7 rangefinder, 43 mm lens, 1/125 f 16, Velvia ISO 100).*

### 📷 QUICK TIP

- Unusual combinations of colours can be generated from the colour wheel when taking colours at the points of a triangle (triad) or rectangle (tetrad). Some triads and tetrads work better than others.
- Make colour an important consideration when you are composing photographs — there are a plethora of stunning colours in our world.

Picking unusual colour combinations, such as those on the left of the diagram below can, at first glance, appear jarring to the eye, but if they are just touches of two colours enhancing the third, a pleasing effect can result. I believe this is particularly true in decoration and attire. The colour contrasts to the right in the diagram below are more usually found and are very eye-catching. Often these colour combinations are used in advertising or web design.

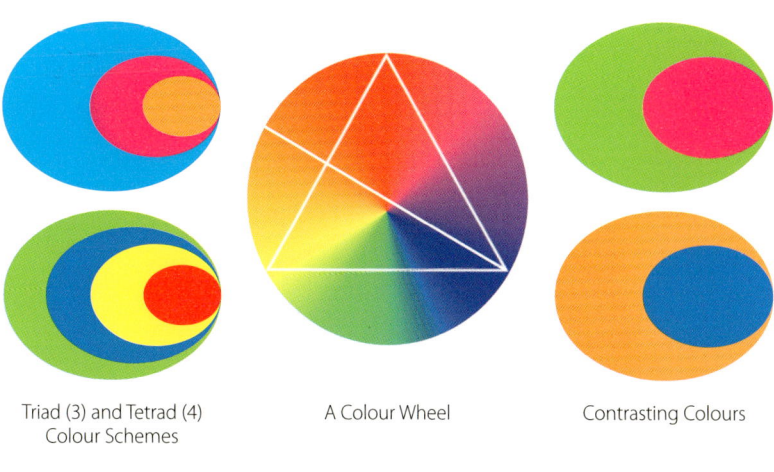

Triad (3) and Tetrad (4) Colour Schemes

A Colour Wheel

Contrasting Colours

**Above:** Sometimes nature presents us with an array of complementary colours. In this case, the view from Mt Buller in Victoria was enhanced by a hazy sky *(6 x 7 rangefinder, 500 mm lens, 1/250 f5.6, Velvia ISO 100)*.

# Dominant Colour

As soon as a photographer raises a camera to his or her eye, it becomes obvious that colour is an important communicator, even before elements such as form, texture, pattern and shape are taken into account. Sometimes, careful positioning can ensure that a colour within the frame very powerfully conveys an emotion.

The interplay of colour can create optical illusions — colour vibration for instance — and to control the outcome you need to consider each colour. If there are too many colours in the frame, there is a struggle for dominance. Remove the struggle and the communication becomes more direct.

**Above:** Every city in Australia has native botanical gardens, and during the spring flowering the gardens are great places to photograph bushscapes splashed with colour. Here in Kings Park in Perth, WA, during the Wildflower Festival, thousands come to take pictures of the dramatic western wildflowers *(6 x 7 rangefinder, 90 mm lens, 1/125 f5.6, Velvia ISO 100)*.

**Opposite, clockwise from top left:** Even though Chambers Pillar, NT, represents a small part of the landscape, its dominant colour immediately draws the eye to it *(35 mm SLR, 15 mm lens, 1/15 f11, Kodachrome ISO 64, tripod)*; Australia's most spectacular water plant, the Lotus Lily, seen here in isolation, brings immediate attention due to its dominance in colour *(35 mm SLR, 80–400 mm zoom lens, 1/125 f8, Velvia ISO 100)*; Australia's most famous landscape, Uluru, stands in stark contrast to a stormy grey sky *(6 x 7 rangefinder, 500 mm lens, 1/125 f5.6, Velvia ISO 100)*.

## 📷 QUICK TIP

- Pictures can be full of impact when one colour outweighs the rest.
- The dominant colour does not have to fill the frame. An image may possess only a small area of the strong colour.
- Rural landscapes, especially when combined in part with natural landscapes, may provide that special splash of dominant colour you are looking for.

# Monochromatic Colour

Monochromatic images use shades of one colour. The term is most often used for black and white or sepia photographs, but it may be applied to any base colour. I believe monochromatic colour can be as pleasing and dramatic to the eye as a combination of vivid colours. The natural world can impart a mood of calm, gentleness and relaxation — quite the opposite to what really goes on in a world of "survival of the fittest". Nonetheless, I believe we treasure the notion as opposed to our chaotic urban existences. Monochromatic photography can convey that mood very effectively.

**Above:** Photographing from a helicopter during late afternoon light has presented a monochromatic image of tonal ranges that, a mere sixty minutes earlier, were a smorgasbord of reds, yellow and blues *(35 mm SLR, 80–200 mm zoom lens, 1/500 f 5.6, Kodachrome ISO 64)*.

**Opposite, top:** A misty morning near the Three Sisters Lookout, Katoomba, NSW *(6 x 6 rangefinder, 60 mm lens, 1/125 f 5.6, Velvia ISO 100)*. **Opposite, bottom:** Descending from the Victorian Alps at dawn I encountered this spectacular layered mountainscape, complete with misty valleys *(35 mm SLR, 80–200 mm zoom lens, 1/500 f 5.6, Kodachrome ISO 64)*.

### 📷 QUICK TIP

- There is less visual information to disturb the mood than in a multi-coloured image and this is why monochromatic photographs communicate more directly and powerfully.

- Monochromatic photographs are more readily taken in overcast weather or during the late or early morning light.

# The Art of Play

The idea of introducing play into my work started to come to the fore in my life when I was in my thirties. A friend gave me a little book by the late Desiderius Orban, artist, philosopher and teacher. His book was entitled, *What is art all about?* and my friend had inscribed it with the words "read between the lines". In this book, Orban states, "competitiveness and the desire for success should be eliminated." He goes on to say, "If the play brings results without conscious effort, that is excellent". This stopped me dead in my tracks, and I began to understand Orban's idea that art was about a process, not about the preconceived notion of an end result. Over the following years, I began to create special times when I could be more playful with my approach to photography — to make images that were more meaningful to me. Whether I used them in my professional work was irrelevant. As a by-product, "playing" with my camera gave me the added benefit of furthering my technical abilities.

What I learned about play was a real wake-up call. With this shift in attitude, I started photographing children at play. Most of my subjects were bush kids, whose play was quite different from what I'd observed of city kids. These children have the dirt beneath their feet and a big, blue sky overhead. They have birds and kangaroos, dad's horses and cattle. Natural visual stimulation surrounds them and overflows into their playtime artwork. As I watched, I could see clearly what Orban was talking about.

### 📷 QUICK TIP

- Suggestions for play — remember that play is not work. It is something totally enjoyable. Play with your camera, take a playful approach to photography, then play with the images you make. Watch children at play and then reach deep down to the carefree and wilder spirit within. Drown your senses in the natural world and get completely lost. Try not to think about anyone else's opinion. Try not to see the picture framed and hanging on the wall. In my business, if other people do not like my "play" then they won't buy it, and that will hurt! Nonetheless, I still play, making time for it whenever I can, and where I cannot use it in my publications, I keep it just for me. And that is all that matters.

Children play and create art from their subconscious, interpreting their experiences through their choice of colour and design. The marks they make are all theirs and quite frankly, they do not care about what the kids next to them are doing. I wish to feel as they do when I photograph.

**Above, left and opposite:** These images were all made over the same period in an attempt to make photographs that portrayed a range of human emotions. The project was for a book and each image was accompanied by a poem. The above image is entitled "Letting Go", the left one "Time", and the one on the opposite page "Joy". Moving the camera during a long exposure, in a different way for each, helped create the images. While each source — a waterfall, a forest and a strangler fig — played a part in stimulating the process of image-making, none of the sources were actually relevant, but simply provided the light and shade, colour, form and texture with which to work *(35 mm SLR, 24 mm lens, 1/10 f 16, Kodachrome ISO 64).*

# After the Field Trip

The technology used to reproduce images for print has advanced in leaps and bounds in recent years. Laborious techniques of the past have been rapidly overtaken and nowadays, digital or film images can be prepared on a modest home computer system. The sophistication of the hardware and software available to the amateur today, is on par with high end professional equipment accessible only five years ago.

If you wish to go beyond having your film developed or digital images processed by a laboratory, it is necessary to acquire some knowledge of the post-photographic-exposure digital world (known as post-production). With the explosion in popularity of digital cameras, the internet has almost become a giant photo album. There is a plethora of photo sharing sites for you to upload your images to share with the world at large.

You can mix still images with video and produce your own DVD (Digital Versatile [or Video] Disc) for screening. Gone are the static images in slide shows of yesteryear, with modern software you can create dynamic effects, panning and zooming across your photos to recreate a journey or convey the mood. Sharing images aside, you can correct any faults in images, manipulate them in many ways, including making them look like paintings. The opportunities for creative expression are as limitless as your imagination.

If you are an advanced amateur photographer, wishing to market your work, then some knowledge of digital technologies is essential in this modern world of electronic communication.

## PRINT RESOLUTION GUIDE

The table below is a rough guide to the final print size you can expect to achieve from a digital camera.

| CAMERA RESOLUTION | PRINT SIZE | | | | | |
|---|---|---|---|---|---|---|
| | 4x6" | 5x7" | 8x10" | 11x14" | 16x20" | 20x30" |
| 2 Megapixel | Photo Quality | Photo Quality | Very Good | Acceptable | Acceptable | Poor |
| 3 Megapixel | Photo Quality | Photo Quality | Excellent | Good | Acceptable | Acceptable |
| 4 Megapixel | Photo Quality | Photo Quality | Photo Quality | Very Good | Good | Acceptable |
| 5 Megapixel | Photo Quality | Photo Quality | Photo Quality | Excellent | Very Good | Very Good |
| 6 Megapixel | Photo Quality | Photo Quality | Photo Quality | Photo Quality | Excellent | Very Good |
| 7 Megapixel | Photo Quality | Photo Quality | Photo Quality | Photo Quality | Excellent | Excellent |
| 8 Megapixel | Photo Quality | Photo Quality | Photo Quality | Photo Quality | Photo Quality | Excellent |
| 10 Megapixel + | Photo Quality | Photo Quality | Photo Quality | Photo Quality | Photo Quality | Photo Quality |

## FILE FORMATS

When working with photographs it is important to always maintain the highest quality, and that being said working with TIFF files is the best option for correction and reproduction.

Shooting in JPEG format is fine, and may be the only option you have. It is important to know though — when you open, modify, then save that image as a JPEG you are effectively throwing information away. This is due to the compression algorithms used in the JPEG format (these are lossy, meaning that information is lost). If you shoot in JPEG, best practice is to open and correct your image in your chosen photo editor and then save as a TIFF file. This ensures you will always have the best available image ready to use for any purpose. If you need to email or upload to a website, saving a copy as a JPEG will yeild beautiful results. Most software will now have specific options for converting images to certain sizes for web or email output.

**JPEG:** A format that loses quality in compression when some information is lost and cannot be reclaimed. Perfect for email and the web. Small file size, good image quality with lossy compression.

**TIFF:** The best option for long term storage of images that you plan to correct. Large file size, excellent image quality with lossless compression.

**RAW:** Not all cameras will have this file format. This format is essentially the raw image data captured by the camera. Better results can be achieved shooting in RAW, but time post-shoot is needed to make your images look the best. Specialised software is also needed to read and convert the RAW file format. This is supplied with the camera. You would always save this file as a TIFF.

## BACKUP YOUR IMAGES

One important aspect post-shoot is to backup your files. It is a horrible process if your hard drive should fail and you have to re-build the operating system, let alone if you have lost all of your digital photographs.

There are many solutions and various ways to do this, CD, DVD, online, etc. External hard disks are the easiest and cheapest (over time) solution. For under $250 you can now purchase a 500 gigabyte (GB) drive. This is large enough to store tens of thousands of images.

Backing up your images needs to become a habit. Every week or post-shoot, connect your backup drive and copy your entire pictures folder to it. Some external drives come with software that can automate this process. Disconnect the drive and place in a safe place. If something should happen to your computer, all that needs reinstalling is software, your irreplaceable photos are safe.

# Digital Manipulation

Once the image is on your computer screen there are many ways to alter it. In fact, digital manipulation is an art form in its own right. You can manipulate colour, crop, soften, brighten, and create a multitude of effects.

In my publishing work, the editing is performed by either a designer or by the pre-press (or film) house that produces high quality scans on a drum scanner and prepares the final publication for the printing press. Designers and pre-press people are highly skilled in the operation and management of these processes.

Even though you may not have developed skills with editing suites, it only takes a little practice to prepare images for general emailing, internet or digital print formats. I always maintain that the more appreciation you have for every aspect of publishing, the more likely you are to excel. If you find the product manuals confusing, there are many courses of study to take.

When a non-digital image is prepared for publication it must be scanned. This image then may require additional preparation, particularly in terms of brightness, contrast and colour adjustment. Where possible, this refining is kept to a minimum — any work done at this stage incurs correction costs. What to correct is often a matter of opinion and is usually directed by a designer or art director. Skillful management of this phase requires considerable experience and can make the difference between a top quality and ordinary publication.

**BRIGHTNESS AND CONTRAST**

It is possible to lighten every pixel in the image or to lighten or darken sections of the image using the controls available in the editing software (above pictures).

**COLOUR CORRECTION**

Colours may be altered by controls or levels depending upon whether you want an overall effect or a single hue manipulated. Remember, variations in colour occur between monitors, printers, and film.

**BLEMISHES**

A sample colour or section may be duplicated from another part of the image then copied over an unwanted mark or object.

## PHOTO-EDITING SOFTWARE

There are many photo-editing software applications available, from simple to sophisticated. Some computer packages include a selection of general applications which may be useful, at least initially. It is a good place to start before investing in a full suite. Next, you might try shareware. Type "shareware photo-editing software" into your search engine. It is surprising what is out there. Later you may wish to invest in a more specialised editing package to experiment and create exciting images.

Aperture™ and Lightroom™, available from Apple and Adobe respectively, are sophisticated digital image management tools that have many functions. These applications not only catalogue and colour correct your digital or scanned photos, but have many other sophisticated functions for sharing your photos with others.

## CROPPING

Cropping is used to fit an image into a particular area, or to change the emphasis of the original image (see page 76). Some photographs lack good composition in the first place and may be dramatically enhanced through skilful cropping. This aspect of manipulation is something that can be creatively stimulating and, with practice, you may well find that your approaches to composition in the field

are influenced by it. Cropping is used extensively in the production of photographic spreads when images must fit together and the entire spread must illustrate one or more predetermined concepts.

# Sharing Your Photos on the Internet

The most effective way to share images quickly with friends is by email. When you attach a small JPEG file to an email, you are sending a glimpse of your life — events, people, special moments — that may range from the trivial to the momentous. To share your images more widely and efficiently, consider creating a website to display the best selection.

The simplest site is one where internet space and templates for your text and images are provided by the host. They are often free but part of the deal could be that there will be advertising on your web page. A more sophisticated option follows.

### AN ONLINE PHOTO-IMAGE GALLERY

Look at various online galleries for ideas. They often show thumbnails (small versions) of their best images which you click to have the low-resolution image enlarged for a proper look. If someone downloaded your image, the resolution would not be sufficient to allow them to print it, which gives you some copyright protection against theft of images. You can always write a note on your site for interested people to contact you if they wish to buy an image.

From within your photo gallery it is possible to provide:

- Screensavers and screen images created from images downloaded from your site, as long as the file size you have prepared is adequate for the screen enlargement.
- Video clips, prepared from digital video so that a viewer can watch a small presentation. This does require that viewers have good modem connection-speed.
- Clip-art of small (usually less than 50 kb) picture files, often etches, that can be easily downloaded.
- eGreetings, though these require HTML coding skills. If you do not have the necessary coding skills, it is possible to provide an HTML tag on your site that will allow a third party to manage eGreetings for you.

The opportunities to display images on a website are boundless and browsing through some of the many interesting sites will give you lots of ideas. Try typing "photo gallery" into your search engine.

# Audio Visual Presentations

You can gain exposure for your work in many ways. For instance, you could approach organisations that support the local community and discuss how you might work together, possibly in a fundraising or community-awareness synergy. If there are several photographers who would like to be involved in exhibiting their work, (perhaps members of a photography club or a group that shares a common interest in a photographic theme) you could gain support from one or a number of local businesses in hosting the event. Just be aware that this kind of activity has to be planned thoroughly and you must make yourself aware of any obligations or responsibilities you might be taking on.

Any of these activities could give your presentation an edge:

- Ask local musicians to perform live to your projected images.
- If one of you is a poet or writer, consider a short reading during the presentation.
- Your presentation could be given a theme that will attract the attention of the media and that, in turn, will promote your show.
- Consider asking a local identity to be MC for the evening.

## PUTTING ON A MULTIMEDIA SHOW

As time passes and your collection of images grows, or after you have returned from an exciting trip with dozens of great images, you will most likely want to share them with others. A very gratifying way to do this is in an evening showing. Slide presentations played a major role in my development as a photographer, naturalist and, most certainly, public speaker. I lacked self-confidence at the beginning but soon learnt to overcome my fears during public presentations of my work. Slides are shown in the dark, and I found that it was easier to speak about the images in the comforting shadows than with lights on, standing in front of an audience.

Consider adding some drama to a presentation by having an opening sequence and a closing set of images set to music, or including video footage.

# Glossary

**ANGLE OF VIEW** The extent of the view taken in by a lens, determined by the focal length of the lens.

**APERTURE** A metal diaphragm through which a controlled amount of light passes to expose the film.

**BACKLIGHT** Light that comes from behind the subject and towards the camera lens — the subject may stand out in silhouette.

**BRACKETING** The technique of taking a number of photographs of the same subject, in quick sequence, at progressive levels of exposure.

**COMPACT CAMERA** A small automated camera with a fixed lens and direct vision viewfinder.

**COMPOSITION** The arrangement of the elements, the subject and other objects, in a scene or photograph.

**DEPTH OF FIELD** The distance between the nearest and farthest objects that appear in acceptably sharp focus in a photograph.

**DIFFUSE LIGHTING** Lighting that is low or moderate in contrast.

**EXPOSURE** The quantity of light allowed to pass through to the film.

**EXTENSION TUBE** A metal or plastic tube inserted between the lens and the camera, making the lens-to-film distance greater.

**FAST FILM** Film with an emulsion that is very sensitive to light.

**FILL-IN** An extra light source, such as flash, used to soften shadows caused by a brighter main light, which may be the sun.

**FILTER** Transparent material placed over a lens to alter the nature, colour or quality of the light passing through it.

**FLASH** An artificial light source (a flashbulb or electronic flash unit) which illuminates a subject being photographed.

**FLASH MEMORY CARD** A storage medium used by most digital cameras. It substitutes for the film in conventional photography.

**FOCAL LENGTH** The distance between the film plane and the optical centre of the lens when the lens is focused at infinity.

**FOCUS** Adjustment of the setting of the focal length to sharply define the selected area of the scene or subject.

**FOCUS LOCK** A lever, button or switch that locks either the lens or body focus, depending on the type of camera.

**FORMAT** The size of the image area on a roll or sheet of film.

**F-STOP** A number that indicates the size of the aperture, hence the amount of light allowed to pass through the lens to the film.

**IMAGE RESOLUTION** The number of dots per inch (dpi) or pixels per inch (ppi) displayed in the printed length in an image.

**ISO** International Standards Organisation. The speed rating for photographic film — representing the film's sensitivity to light. A higher ISO number indicates the film is more sensitive and requires less light for a proper exposure.

**JPEG** Joint Photographic Experts Group.

**LCD** Liquid Crystal Display. A method of displaying data continuously by means of a liquid-crystal film, sealed between glass plates, which changes its optical properties when a voltage is applied.

**LENS** A single piece of transparent material with at least one curved surface that is used to change the convergence of light rays.

**LENS PERSPECTIVE** Provides linear perspective, or the sense of depth and distance, in a two-dimensional photograph.

**LENS SPEED** The widest aperture (smallest f-stop) in relation to focal length at which a lens can be set. A fast lens transmits more light than a slow lens.

**LINEAR PERSPECTIVE** A geometrical system for showing the apparent positions and magnitudes of objects to give the illusion of space and distance on a flat surface.

**LONG LENS** See telephoto lens.

**MACRO LENS** A lens that has continuous focusing capacity from infinity to 1:2 and extreme life-size 1:1 close-ups.

**MATRIX METERING** Light coming from a subject passes through the lens into a multi-segment light meter. The camera sets aperture and shutter speed for the optimal exposure.

**MEDIUM FORMAT** A film (and camera) format providing a larger and better image than 35 mm size, suitable for commercial reproduction. The most popular sizes are 6×6 cm, 6×4.5 cm and 6×7 cm.

**MONOPOD** A one-legged support used to hold the camera steady.

**MOTOR DRIVE** An electronic mechanism for advancing the film to the next frame and resetting the shutter. Popular for action-sequence photography.

**MULTI-PATTERN METERING** For metering accurate exposure across unevenly lit subjects by dividing a scene into a matrix of separate cells. Each can be metered independently to accurately calculate exposure when highlights and shadows exist outside the centre of the frame.

**OVER-EXPOSE** To set exposure so that too much light reaches the film, resulting in a dense negative or a light, washed-out transparency.

**PANNED/PANNING** To move continuously while shooting, to record on film a panorama, or to keep a moving person or object in view.

**PANORAMA** A broad view across a continuous expanse of the horizon.

**PERSPECTIVE** The visual representation of the three dimensions of depth and distance in a two-dimensional photograph.

**PIXEL** A single picture element of a digital photo. In a digital image each pixel is assigned a location and colour value.

**PIXELATED** An image blurred by enlarging certain pixels and reducing the resolution.

**RANGEFINDER** A viewfinder included on many cameras as an aid in composing and, in some cases, focusing. Can cause parallax distortion.

**RAW** A file format containing the uncorrected image data captured by the camera sensor.

**REFLECTOR** Any surface from which light can be reflected on to a subject, usually into areas of shadow.

**RESOLUTION** The fineness of detail recorded in a photographic image or print.

**SATURATION** The perception of colour according to whether it displays more or less hue and brightness.

**SCANNER** A scanner is a device that captures analogue data (e.g., an image) and converts it to digital data, for input into a computer to display, edit, store, or output.

**SHUTTER SPEED** The amount of time for which the shutter stays open to light, measured in fractions of a second.

**SLOW LENS** A lens with a small maximum aperture (e.g., f8). The lens lets in less light, necessitating longer exposure times in low light.

**SLR** Single Lens Reflex. A camera of 35 mm or medium format, in which a system of mirrors and prisms allows the viewing of a scene through the same lens that takes the picture.

**SPOT METER** A narrow-angle exposure meter that takes reflected light readings from a small area of a subject, and can be used some distance away.

**STANDARD LENS** A lens produces an image similar to the original scene as perceived by the human eye. It has a focal length approximately equal to the diagonal of the film format (e.g., 50 mm for a 35 mm camera). Also called a normal lens.

**TELEPHOTO LENS** A lens with a focal length much greater than the diagonal of the film format (or standard lens) which is used e.g., 300 mm on 35 mm format, when standard is 50 mm. Showing an enlarged section with a narrower angle of view than a standard lens. Depth of field decreases as focal length increases. Can isolate a subject from a distance. Also called a long lens.

**TIFF** Tagged Image File Format.

**TTL** Through the Lens. A type of camera that allows TTL metering and focusing.

**TWILIGHT** The time just before sunrise or just after sunset when the sky is lit by the sun's light but the sun is not visible.

**UV FILTER** A clear, colourless filter that absorbs ultra-violet radiation.

**VIEWPOINT** The position (above, below, far or near) relative to a photographic subject, from which a shot is made.

**WIDE-ANGLE LENS** A lens with a shorter focal length and a wider angle of view than a standard lens; focal length is less than the diagonal of the film frame. In 35 mm photography, lenses 24–35 mm are thought of as wide-angles, and those under 24 mm as ultra-wide. Depth of field increases as focal length decreases. Also called a short lens.

**ZOOM LENS** A lens of continuously variable focal length; in effect, many lenses of different focal lengths in one unit (e.g. 80-200 mm). Also called a variable focus lens.

# Index

**A**
animal 16

**B**
background 21, 38, 50, 56, 58, 60–62, 68, 72, 80, 82
backlighting 42, 43
balance 48, 50, 51, 90
Blue Mountains 22, 23, 57
Bungle Bungle Ranges 13

**C**
camera 4, 6, 7, 17, 18, 25, 26, 28, 31, 32, 34, 40, 44, 46, 47, 54, 60, 62, 66, 67, 76, 77, 80, 84, 90, 96, 100, 101, 102, 112
digital 6, 90, 112
SLR 6
Cape Hillsborough NP 82, 89
Cape Leeuwin 25
centre-weighted metering adjustment 42
clouds 28
colour 4, 12, 18, 30, 38, 46, 52, 54, 64, 66, 78, 90, 92–96, 98, 100–105
colour wheel 95
content 10
Cradle Mountain 18
cropping 76, 88, 105

**E**
exposure 26, 42, 62, 66, 88, 101, 102, 107

**F**
Fitzgerald River NP 65
foreground 24, 32, 48, 50, 58, 61, 67, 72, 81
frame 17, 26, 30, 38, 50, 58, 62, 77, 80, 96
Fraser Island 4, 74, 81

**G**
GIF 103
Goold Island NP 90

**H**
Hamersley Range 60
Hamilton Island 90
helicopter 34, 68, 98
Heron Island 27
Horizon 48
horizontals 18
Hotham Heights 82
human form 18

**I**
ISO setting 44, 80

**J**
Jim Jim Falls 30
JPEG 103, 106

**K**
Kakadu National Park 15, 18, 30, 38
Kata Tjuta 4, 56, 59, 64, 77, 82
Katherine Gorge 32
Kings Canyon Gorge 75
Kings Park 96

**L**
LCD screen 6
lens
macro 6, 8
standard 8, 20, 70, 103
telephoto 8, 15, 16, 20, 30, 58, 66
wide-angle 8, 15, 20, 21, 40, 56, 58, 65
light 4, 18, 20–28, 30, 31, 32, 34, 36, 38, 40–44, 46, 53, 56, 59, 62, 78, 79, 81, 84, 85, 86, 88, 90, 94, 98, 101
light meter readings 31
lightning 28
Lord Howe Island 72

**M**
Mary River 64
monochromatic colour 98
monopod 8
mood 4, 10, 15, 22, 27, 30, 38, 98
Mt Buller 95
Mulga woodland 4

**N**
Nambung NP 57, 72
Natural Arch 59
Northern Territory Wildlife Park 89
North Stradbroke Island 32, 58

**O**
online photo-image gallery 106
Ormiston Gorge 43

**P**
pattern 26, 30, 31, 53, 54, 64, 65, 96
peripheral 66
photo-editing 105
photography
digital 4, 6, 8, 16, 20, 22, 24, 25, 30, 37, 40, 47, 48, 62, 70, 82, 90, 92, 98, 100, 102, 107, 111
natural light 24–26, 32, 38, 40
underwater 27, 32, 38, 40, 41

Photoshop 42, 62
PICT 103
picture composition 46
pixel 102–104
plants 20, 21
Polaroid filter 34
Port Campbell 4, 27
proportion 74

**R**
rain 4, 22, 28, 38, 90
resolution 6, 8, 102, 103, 106

**S**
self-timer 44, 74
shade 32, 78, 79, 94, 101
shadow 30, 34, 42, 43, 54, 80, 86, 112
shutter speed 4, 21, 32, 34, 44, 62
SLR 4, 6, 13, 18, 23, 27, 28, 30, 34, 38, 44–46, 53, 57, 62, 64, 65, 74, 75, 80, 82, 85, 96, 98, 101, 112
Stirling Ranges 53
storm 25, 28, 52
Sturt's Stony Desert 13
subjects 15, 25, 44, 49, 50, 51, 56, 60, 74, 82, 86, 100
sun 12, 15, 21, 22, 25–28, 32, 34, 36, 40–44, 61, 66, 78, 82, 86

**T**
Tarkine 28
tetrad 94
TIFF 103
topography 12, 24
Townsville Town Common 37
triad 94
tripod 7, 8, 21, 28, 32, 44, 48, 49, 60–62, 72, 74, 88, 96
Twelve Apostles 27, 37

**U**
Uluru-Kata Tjuta National Park 4, 21
UV filters 34

**V**
verticals 18
viewfinder 10, 54, 66, 68

**W**
Warrumbungle NP 42
Wave Rock 18, 80
William Day NP 75

# Online reading

Visit our dedicated Photograph Australia Website: www.photographaustralia.com.au and join our forum. Visit the site which includes interesting features such as an interactive map and extensive photo tips covering every aspect of photography in Australia. You will meet other keen photographers where you will be able to exchange ideas. Take advantage of the opportunity to enter our Photo of the Week competition!

Browse the internet and view the work of Australia's leading wildlife photographers.

Wilderness Landscape Photography of Australia, Robert Rankin www.rankin.com.au

Fine art Australian landscape photographer, Anthony Roach presents his evocative seascapes of the east coast of Australia featuring images of Coogee Beach www.anthonyroach.com.au

Thirdglance is the online gallery of James Pierce's panoramic landscape photography of southern Australia www.thirdglance.com

Tasmanian and Australian Fine Art landscape photography by Richard Newton's Australian Island Imaging www.islandimaging.com

ANZANG Nature and Landscape Photographer of the Year Competition www.anzangnature.com

Unique and amazing Australian nature and landscape photography
www.photoshopaustralia.com

Scott Haskins Photography — landscape photography
www.scotthaskinsphotography.com

Award Winning Photography by Hendro Soetrisno www.seeinglandscape.com

Antarctic Photography by Doug Thost
www.dougthost.com

South Australian landscape photographer ozscapes www.petedobre.com.au

Breathtaking Australian panoramic landscape photography by Mark Gray
www.landscapephotography.com.au

Australian landscape photography by Ian Wallace www.ianwallace.com.au

Ken Duncan is famous for his landscape photography of Australia, panoramic photo and limited edition prints www.kenduncan.com

Sam Burns Gallery, fresh, creative Australian photography www.samburns.com.au

Spectacular landscape photography from all over Australia - prints, books, gifts, digital photography tips www.nickrains.com

Inspiring Australian panoramic landscape photography by Andrew Brown
www.abscenes.com

Specialising in Australian panoramic landscape photography www.tonyfeder.com

Large format, fine art, landscape and nature photography of Australia
www.jeremydaalder.com

Red Earth Photographics - Central Australian landscape photography
www.redearthphotographics.com.au

Landscape and wilderness photography
www.robblakers.com

Tim Ruckley Landscape Photography
www.timruckley.com

## PHOTOGRAPHIC DETAILS

I began my career using only medium format cameras, 6x6 Yashica, Rolliflex and Hasselblad. I then changed to Nikon 35 mm SLR and later started using 35 mm for flowers and animals. I chose to use 6x7 and 6x17 for landscapes. Now, with the major development of digital cameras and the software for post-production, I exclusively use digital SLR cameras, (shown as DSLR in the captions). I share this with you as nothing more than a point of interest because camera brands, models of cameras and so on don't make my pictures, I do! For you, the approach to these issues is entirely personal and has more to do with opportunity, budget and of course the requirements you have for the end use.

## DISCLAIMER:

*Where brand names are mentioned in this book the reader should in no way consider it an endorsement of the product. Steve Parish Publishing does not endorse any commercial products, processes, or services. The views and opinions of the author may not be used for advertising or product endorsement purposes.*

*The author and Steve Parish Publishing do not warrant or assume any legal liability or responsibility for the accuracy, completeness, or usefulness of any information, apparatus, product, or process disclosed.*

Published by Steve Parish Publishing Pty Ltd
PO Box 1058, Archerfield, Qld 4108 Australia
**www.steveparish.com.au**
© Steve Parish Publishing

All rights reserved. No part of this publication may be reproduced, stored in a retrieval system, or transmitted in any form or by any means, electronic, mechanical, photocopying, recording or otherwise, without the prior permission in writing of the publisher.

ISBN 9781741933314

First published 2008

Principal photographer: Steve Parish

Additional photography: Greg Harm, SPP: pp. 5 (top), 8, 37 (top) & 104

Map, p. 12 by MAPgraphics Pty Ltd, Brisbane, Australia

Photographs of equipment generously supplied by: Canon Australia Pty Ltd (Canon IXUS 85), Maxwell Optical Industries Pty Ltd (Nikon)

Adobe product screen shots reprinted with permission from Adobe Systems Incorporated.

Front cover image: MacDonnell Ranges

Title page main image: Flinders Ranges Inset, top to bottom: Uluru; Close-up claypan detail and leafless shrub shadow within Rainbow Valley

Text: Steve Parish
Design: Gill Stack, SPP
Editing: Kerry McDuling, Ted Lewis, Sarah Lowe; Michele Perry & Helen Anderson, SPP
Production: Tina Brewster, SPP

Prepress by Colour Chiefs Digital Imaging, Brisbane, Australia
Printed in Singapore by Imago

**Produced in Australia at the Steve Parish Publishing Studios**